AF668442

Lata Mangeshkar

...in her own voice

Lata Mangeshkar

...in her own voice

Conversations with

Nasreen Munni Kabir

NIYOGI
BOOKS

Published by
NIYOGI BOOKS
Block D, Building No. 77,
Okhla Industrial Area, Phase-I,
New Delhi-110 020, INDIA
Tel: 91-11-26816301, 26818960
Email: niyogibooks@gmail.com
Website: www.niyogibooksindia.com

Text © Lata Mangeshkar/Nasreen Munni Kabir
Photographs © Lata Mangeshkar Collection
Sanjeev Kohli Collection
Rachana Shah Collection
S.N. Gourisaria Collection
Hyphen Films Collection

Black and white photograph (pp.70) of painting is by M.R. Achrekar

In the event that inadvertently the name of an individual photographer has been uncredited, Niyogi Books would be happy to include this information on notification by the concerned individual in subsequent editions, if any.

Design: Shaju K Anthony
ISBN: 978-93-89136-31-9

Year of Publication: May 2009
2nd Impression: July 2009
Revised Edition (Flexi back): 2019

All rights are reserved. No part of the publication may be reproduced or transmitted in any form or by any means, electronic or mechanical, including photocopying, recording or by any information storage and retrieval system without the written permission and consent of the Publisher.

Printed at: Niyogi Offset Pvt. Ltd., New Delhi, India

मेरे प्रिय बाबा और प्रिय माई को

अर्पण

लता

Dedicated to my dear Baba and Mai

— Lata

Lata Mangeshkar's most striking features are her sparkling eyes and disarming smile.

Introduction

Lata Mangeshkar remembers a dream that returned to her every night when she was in her early twenties. Coming home from recording two songs in the morning, two in the afternoon, and two in the evening, she would fall asleep and the dream unfurled: it is early morning and she finds herself all alone at a black-stoned temple by the sea. Unaware of the deity associated with the temple, she makes her way through the sacred space. At the back of the temple, there is a door. She opens it and sees a few steps leading from the door to the dappled water. She sits on the stone steps and the waves gently wash over her feet.

Young Lata thought nothing of the dream but when it reoccurred night after night, and for several months, she decided to share it with her mother, Shudhhamati Mangeshkar, who listened quietly to her and said: 'God has blessed you. You will be very famous one day.'

Her mother's reading of the dream could not have been more prophetic. Today Lata Mangeshkar is loved to the point of worship. People speak of her voice as a divine gift and some even talk of her being an avatar of the Goddess Saraswati. She is acclaimed as one of India's greatest singers, has won countless awards, including the Dada Saheb Phalke Award (1989) and received extraordinary recognition, including India's highest civilian honour, the Bharat Ratna, in 2001.

Lata Mangeshkar's fame in the world of Indian music is unrivalled. Unlike many stars whose celebrity status distances them from ordinary people, admiration for her is highly personalised because she is intimately linked to the emotions of millions of people through her songs. No bond could be stronger.

Since 1949, when she was first noticed for her extraordinary singing talent in the song 'Aayega aanewala' from the film *Mahal*, Lata Mangeshkar's voice has taken firm hold of the Indian imagination. The haunting and timeless quality of the song itself — brought alive through the tuneful purity of her voice and flawless phrasing — had an instant and profound impact on all who heard it. For countless millions, Lata Mangeshkar continues to embody an emotional experience through her solos and duets with Mohammed Rafi, Kishore Kumar or Mukesh. Her songs transcend all barriers of language, region and religion — and her spirituality is present in equal measure whether she is singing a *bhajan* or a *naat*.

For decades, she was the most sought-after singer, and every top actress, from Nargis, Madhubala, Meena Kumari, Nutan to Madhuri Dixit, wanted Lata as their voice. She remains a widely respected figure in the Indian film industry and is affectionately called 'Didi' [elder sister] by

With Nasreen Munni Kabir during the making of Lata In Her Own Voice *(1991). Photo credit: Peter Chappell.*

all. Lata Mangeshkar is the highest-selling Indian artist and has made fortunes for Indian record companies. Her songs have helped spread an appreciation of Hindi film music throughout the world. In India, she has achieved iconic status, and created everlasting music that has become the soundtrack to our lives.

Based on *Lata in Her Own Voice,* a six-part documentary series that I directed in 1991, [produced by Hyphen Films Ltd for Channel 4 TV in the UK; Commissioning Editor: Farrukh Dhondy], this book was set in motion through an email addressed to Sanjeev Kohli, composer Madan Mohan's son. Sanjeev Kohli played a crucial role in the making of *Lata in Her Own Voice* and I sought his advice again to see whether we could preserve in book form the extended interview with Lataji that I had recorded for the film. With characteristic and lightning speed, Sanjeev Kohli emailed back: 'Didi says go ahead.' I then asked whether we could update the material, make it longer, more conversational, and fill in any gaps that might be apparent.

Once I had her agreement to the idea of a 'book of conversations,' I called her several times a week between May and August 2008. We went over the original interview and covered many new areas of discussion. She sometimes talked in English but most often in Hindi. I immediately typed her answers on my laptop, translating them into English.

Lataji was always open, warm and candid. Her memory for songs and dates was astounding. When asked the name of a song she had sung for Ghulam Haider or Naushad, her recall was instant, despite the fact that she has recorded several thousand songs and was being asked to remember something that had taken place over fifty years ago. And when she could not recall a song or a date, she had no hesitation in saying to me: 'I don't remember.'

Sometimes a telephone conversation had a strangely humbling and unnerving effect on me. While discussing 'Aayega aanewala,' when I asked if we could include the beautiful opening lines of the song in our book, she said: 'You need the words? You can write them down.' She then proceeded to hum, half-sing and recite from memory:

Khaamosh hai zamaana chup chaap hain sitaare
Aaram se hai duniya bekal hai dil ke maare
Aise mein koi aahat is tarah aa rahi hai
Jaise ke chal raha ho mann mein koi hamaare
Ya dil dhadak raha hai is aas ke sahaare

Time stands still. The stars are silent
The world is at rest. Yet my heart is uneasy
Suddenly I hear footsteps approaching
As though someone were walking through my heart
Or is it the sound of my heart quickening with hope?

I was too embarrassed to tell Lataji the kind of effect hearing her half-sing, half-recite the poem had on me. Remember, this was Lata Mangeshkar on the line, not a recording! Sitting in my Maida Vale flat on a sunny London day, I felt a rush of emotion, a sense of being an unworthy eavesdropper who happened to hear a bit of living history.

Lata Mangeshkar's songs are living history — so strongly tied to all our life stories and articulating our many emotions. Once the lyrics were typed in, our conversation continued and we talked of other things.

This is how the book slowly took shape: we would talk, I would type and during our next call, I would read back the translated conversation to her and she would say: 'Yes, that's it. But it was in 1945 not '46.'

After a month of phone calls, I wondered why it was so easy to translate Lataji. And then it dawned on me: her voice is so utterly expressive that her tone dictated the most fitting word to use. You knew when 'resigned' — as in 'Lataji said in a resigned tone' was right — and when 'meekly' painted a more accurate picture of how she reacted at a particular moment. Lataji expresses subtle shades of meaning — emotional and psychological — and so for the attentive listener nothing is lost. It is this gift of being expressive that comes through her voice and when

In the late '40s, Master Ghulam Haider had predicted that Lata Mangeshkar's success would reach the skies. Near Kolhapur. 1949. Photo credit: Madhavrao Shinde.

she sings 'Ajeeb dastaan hai ye,' 'Chandni raatein pyaar ki baatein,' 'Ai dilrubaa nazaaren mila,' or 'Lag jaa gale,' she stirs an emotional response.

From a more technical perspective, it made complete sense to me why so many composers have marvelled at Lataji's uncanny ability to instantly grasp both the tune and the emotional import of a song. She is a brilliant actress, and though unseen, her voice adds hugely to the scene's drama and intensity. An actress lives with the character she is playing for many months and so comes to understand how to deliver dialogue and judge the pitch of performance. Lataji is able to grasp in an instant the psychology and emotional map of a character, and like the best male playback singers such as Mohammed Rafi, Kishore Kumar and Mukesh, who have also achieved this, she sings in character. In her voice there is total identification and empathy with the character's depth of feelings.

There are many examples in which we see how Lataji's singing enhances the impact of a scene. Think of Nargis miming 'O mere laal aa ja' in *Mother India* or Meena Kumari in 'Chalte chalte' in *Pakeezah*, or Nutan in 'Suno chhoti si gudiya ki lambi kahaani' in *Seema.* An interesting question to ask is whether Lataji is singing for the actress or the actress's performance is determined by Lataji.

Her musical skill is well known and widely appreciated, but her natural acting talent and her mastery of the intricacies of language and poetry is equally remarkable. During our conversations, she repeatedly said that for her, lyrics were the most important aspect of a song. She has always preferred songs that say something about feelings and are not just catchy tunes.

From September 2008 to March 2009, Lataji and I went through the entire manuscript, page by page, word by word, to avoid any errors that might have been caused by phone crackle. As I read the manuscript to her, she listened with complete attention, gently correcting and elaborating.

There is a deluge of misinformation on Lata Mangeshkar and I found dozens of very imaginative tales on the Net, including one that claimed that Lataji, on hearing that Master Vinayak had died, cried the whole night and then thought Lord Dattatraya was standing before her telling her to be brave and to carry on struggling through life. When I asked her if this had really happened, straightaway Lataji said: 'No, it didn't.'

One of the aims of this book is to try and separate truth and fact from rumour and fabulous myth.

Many accounts of exceptional artists of the past, especially in Indian cinema, depend on hearsay or on the memory of those who knew them. This is particularly true of early film practitioners because so little first-hand written material exists. But memories and impressions of people are subjective, and can be unreliable. We know history is subjective. And what you remember of people sometimes says more about you than them — and so to hear

Lataji speak in such detail about her own life, in her own words, is what makes this book a unique record.

In a single lifespan, Lata Mangeshkar has been and is witness to the astonishing changes in the history of India, and has helped in great measures to redefine the world of Indian film music. She has worked with composers, lyricists, singers, actresses and filmmakers who have together assured the place of Hindi film music in our hearts, potently and powerfully.

This book includes observations by Lataji's immediate family and leading personalities of the Hindi film industry who have described their relationship with her and share what they felt about her singing abilities. Their comments add a greater understanding to the 'Lata Mangeshkar' phenomenon. Many interviews were recorded in 1991 and since that time, some exceptional artists who spoke of her have sadly passed away; these include Naushad Ali, Majrooh Sultanpuri, Sajjad Hussain and Talat Mahmood.

It has been an undoubted privilege for me to work on this book, to spend time with a warm, engaging and caring woman with a brilliant mind. And one who, difficult as it is to believe when you hear her youthful voice, will soon be ninety years old.

Her infectious laugh, lively eyes, sparkling sense of humour and great wisdom are easily the most endearing aspects of her multi-layered personality. The very special quality about her is the respect she commands and the respect she gives. In private she may enjoy impersonating a co-singer or indulge in a little harmless gossip, but in public she will neither put anyone down nor show disrespect in any way. In all our conversations she always spoke of Mohammed Rafi as 'Rafi Sahib,' and of Mukesh as 'Mukesh Bhaiya.'

She is never familiar and keeps a polite distance. But the world around her has changed, and her notions of discretion and privacy are no longer seen as virtues.

Talking of public figures today often means delving into their private lives and digging for dirt rather than simply asking who they are, how they work and what they think. I hope this book — by asking those questions — will shed light on the work and life of the extraordinarily gifted, deeply modest and God-fearing Lata Mangeshkar.

Without the unstinting help and support of Sanjeev Kohli, this book would not exist. Special thanks to Rachana Shah, Peter Chappell, the Mangeshkar family, Javed Akhtar, Dipa Chaudhuri, Navidita Thapa, Madhuparna Banerjee, Akshay Kohli, the Kohli family, Anand Bhosle, Mahesh Rathod, Vijay Jani, Angelina Rodrigues, S.N. Gourisaria, Lindy Sharpe, Ramachandra Guha, Tim Highsted, John Minchinton, Hazel Morgan, Lesley Mason, Gautam Rajadhyaksha, Justin Chubb, Niranjana Rao, Barbara Meyer, and my sisters Priya Kumar and Shameem Kabir for their invaluable support and continued encouragement.

Nasreen Munni Kabir, London

At Shashank Lalachand's recording studio in Bombay. 1991. Photo credit: Peter Chappell.

My father whom we called Baba was a classical music singer and at home we could hear music day and night...

Deenanath Mangeshkar and his wife, Shuddhamati, with their three daughters: Asha (on her mother's lap), the five-year old Lata (right of her father) and Meena. Taken in Sangli in a photographer's studio. Circa *1934.*

LM: Throughout my childhood, I listened to Baba sing and could remember every note, but didn't have the courage to sing in front of him. One day, he was teaching Raag Puriya Dhanashri to a young *shagird* and for some reason, he left the room and Baba's pupil continued singing. I was playing outside and heard him. I had a feeling the boy wasn't singing it right. So I went in and said: 'That isn't it. This is how it should be sung.' And I sang the notes to him. At that moment, my father returned and heard me. He called Mai, my mother, and said: 'We have a good singer at home and we never knew it.'

At six the next morning, Baba woke me saying: 'Take the *tanpura*. You will study singing.' We began with the same *raag* — Puriya Dhanashri. That was the day I started learning how to sing. I think I was about five-years old.

NMK: It is said when you were six, you were singing a song and suddenly became unconscious. And when you woke, you continued singing from the point you left off. Is this true?

LM: No, it isn't! It never happened. *[laughs]*

NMK: Clearly you are mythologised like people who capture the imagination of millions — and so stories about you spread like myths whether true or false. Maybe we must attribute this story, like many others found in great abundance on the Net, as part of 'Lata-lore.' May we start at the beginning? Where were you living in the 1930s?

LM: We were in Sangli, a small trading town in Maharashtra. My father owned a large house with thirteen rooms. We lived on the top floor and the ground floor of the house had been converted into small flats which were rented to different families.

NMK: These were the days of prosperity when your father, Deenanath Mangeshkar, a celebrated singer, stage-actor, and co-producer of musical plays *[sangeet natak]* was considered a leading light of Marathi theatre. Did he run his own theatre company?

LM: Yes. It was called the Balwant Sangeet Mandali and was formed in 1918 when Baba was eighteen. The company was created with his friends Chintamanrao Kolhatkar and Krishnarao Kolhapure, Padmini Kolhapure's grandfather, and whom my paternal aunt later married. Baba was from Mangeshi, a small place in Goa and when he was about eight or nine, his mother sent him to study music under Baba Mashelkar who was in Goa at the time. My father later became a disciple of the Gwalior *gharana*.

NMK: What was the most enjoyable aspect of your singing lessons?

LM: What I liked best was learning how to sing a *bandish* — and I learned as many as I could. I didn't pay as much attention to *sargam* or *alaaps*. I would ask Baba to explain the personality of a *raag* to me. How is this *raag*? How is that *raag*? By God's grace and His blessings, my voice could handle *taan*s and I sang them well.

NMK: How old were you when you first performed in public? How did that come about?

LM: It was in the late 1930s. Baba's theatre company was on tour in Sholapur and one day some people asked him to sing at a concert. I overheard their conversation and asked: 'Baba, can I sing with you?' Laughingly, he replied: 'How will you sing?' 'Why not? I can sing!' So he said: 'Which *raag* will you sing?' 'Khambavati. And two songs as well.' He finally agreed to let me sing on stage.

In our theatre company, we had a harmonium player whom we affectionately called Babi 'Borkar'— from the English 'bore karne wala' [a bore], and a *tabla* player, Ustaad Valya. They accompanied me as I practised for a few days.

The music programme was held at Nutan Theatre in Sholapur and before Baba came on stage, I sang Raag Khambavati followed by two Marathi songs: 'Shura mi vandile' from K.P. Khadilkar's play *Manapaman* and 'Suhasya tujhe manasi mohi' from Prabhakar's play *Brahmakumari*. Then my father sang through the night. I remember falling asleep on the stage with my head in Baba's lap. It was my first public performance. I was nine years old. *[smiles]*

I sang at other concerts with Baba, and when I was eleven, we sang together on the radio.

NMK: Did your father tell you something about singing or music that has helped you through your life?

LM: When I was learning how to sing, I used to make all kinds of excuses. I was very young and preferred to play. I pretended to have a headache or stomach ache. It was always something. I would run from the room where Baba taught me. Sometimes he would catch hold of me and bring me right back. I would protest saying: 'I feel shy to sing in front of you. I'm scared.'

One day Baba sat me down and said: 'I know I'm your father. But a father is like a guru too. Always remember — whether a guru or father is teaching you — when you sing you must think to yourself you will sing better than him. Never think how can I sing in his presence? Remember this. You must excel your guru.'

I have never forgotten Baba's words.

Aged ten, Poona.

NMK: What did your father think of film music?

LM: Film music wasn't hugely appreciated at home. The family preferred classical music. And my father was a very conservative man. He was strict about the way we dressed, we could never wear powder or make-up. We couldn't go out freely. Baba didn't like us going out late at night to watch plays, not even his own productions. He was strict in that way. But that was the norm; this was some seventy years ago.

During our childhood, we lived according to the mores of the time. Mai was from Khandesh and wore the traditional nine-yard saree. She remained a pure vegetarian throughout her life, but cooked non-vegetarian food for my father. My brother Hridaynath and his daughter, Radha, are also vegetarian and don't even eat eggs. But we sisters became non-vegetarian.

Baba didn't like films. We weren't allowed to go to the movies — except for films made by the Marathi filmmaker Bhalji Pendharkar and Calcutta's New Theatres. Baba believed their productions had good music and sensible stories. He always liked Saigal Sahib and so did I. At home I sang his songs, especially 'Ek bangala bane nyaara' from the film *President*.

I was allowed to sing Saigal Sahib's songs at home but no other film songs. Nor did I much care for them.

NMK: Besides working in the theatre, your father also worked in films. Did he enjoy it?

LM: He didn't like the idea of acting in films or singing for them. But he loved the theatre. Those were the days when it was customary for male actors to play female roles on stage. In the 1919 play, *Bhav Bandhan*, Baba played the role of Latika, a spirited modern girl whose personality appealed to him so much that it was said I was renamed Lata — even though I was called 'Hridaya' when I was born. I am not sure in which year I was renamed Lata.

When Baba was very young and working at the Kirloskar Natak Mandali, he even learned *kathak*, and danced in some early plays. He knew Urdu and Farsi [Persian] and one of his great successes was the Urdu play, *Taj-e-Wafa*, produced by the Kirloskar Natak Mandali, which apparently caused a sensation in Calcutta.

Baba was devoted to the theatre but he believed that girls of good families should not work on the stage. But we sisters thought it was an excellent idea!

NMK: How did you finally manage to change his mind?

LM: One day I told Baba: 'There's a young child character who sings in the play *Bhav Bandhan* and I'd like to sing her song.' He reluctantly agreed. I went to the theatre, dressed in my everyday clothes, *[laughs]* sang the song on stage and came home. After that, he didn't encourage me to act again. But I believed it was the right thing to do and the thought never left me.

We were once in Pandharpur touring with our theatre troupe, and when Baba went to Bombay on work, I told Ganapatrao Mohite, a disciple of Baba's, whom we called Ganu Mama: 'I want to play the prince's role in *Punyaprabhaav* because he sings three songs.' Ganu Mama nervously asked: 'What will your father say?' 'You can convince him or try persuading Mai.' So he helped prepare me for the part.

Baba was still in Bombay on the day I performed on stage. I was trembling so badly that two other actors had to hold on to me. *[laughs]* I could barely speak my lines but somehow managed to sing.

The next day my father returned home and heard the whole story. I didn't come out of my room. I was so terrified! Baba always talked to us in Marathi — as you know he was originally from Mangeshi in Goa — and when he was very happy or angry, he spoke in Konkani. He came inside the room and said: 'Phuttur mage le!' [Doomed is my fate]. I started crying and couldn't say a word.

Mai calmed him down by saying: 'She's only a child. Let her have her way.' Baba didn't say another word to me. I don't know what came over him, but soon after that, he asked the playwright Kothiwale, who had previously worked with him, to write a children's play for me. Kothiwale wrote *Gurukul* in which I played Shri Krishna and my sister Meena was Sudama.

NMK: I believe your father was married once before?

LM: Yes. His first wife was Narmada who was also known as 'Mai.' She was the daughter of Seth Haridas Ramdas Laad, a wealthy business family of Thalner in Gujarat. They were married in 1922, but she passed away in childbirth. Their daughter was called Lata and was looked after by my maternal grandmother and my mother. But sadly, the young infant only survived nine months.

From a young age, her spirited and lively nature was apparent to all. At eighteen.

In 1927, my father married my mother who was Narmada's younger sister. She was called Shivanti but was renamed 'Shudhhamati'— the pure mind. Everyone in the family called her 'Mai.'

NMK: I wonder whether you were named 'Lata' in memory of your father's first child or the spirited young 'Latika' of the play *Bhav Bandhan*?

LM: I really don't know the answer.

NMK: Another confusion written about widely is that you were named 'Hema.' Is this right?

LM: No. My father gave me the name 'Hridaya' when I was born. Not Hema.

NMK: That's another erroneous 'fact' widely reported. You were born in Indore in Madhya Pradesh. Were your parents living there at the time? Or was your father on tour in Indore with his theatre troupe?

LM: Baba wasn't present when I was born. I believe he was on tour. My maternal grandmother had gone to visit an aunt of ours who lived in a lane in the Sikh Mohalla, a neighbourhood of Indore. It's customary for the first child in the family to be born in the maternal home — so my mother had gone to Indore to be with my grandmother. That is how I came to be born there on 28 September, 1929. It was a Saturday. I was born at home and the attending doctor was a lady called Dr. Motabai. My sister Meena was also born in Indore in 1931.

NMK: Did you know that you share the same birth date (28th September) with many actors including Marcello Mastrioanni (1924) and Brigitte Bardot (1934)? And the great Chinese philosopher Confucius was also born on the same day in 551 BC.

LM: I didn't know that. *[laughs]*

NMK: In your childhood, were you very close to your sisters?

LM: Yes, we were. We're still close. We love each other very much. We're a close-knit family. We never fight. But we fought a lot when we were children. *[laughs]* I had lots of friends too. I played with all the girls and boys who lived on the ground floor of our house in Sangli.

My games were really terrible. It's the truth. I used to sit inside a car tyre and the girls would roll me down the street. I was really a very naughty child. I climbed trees, picked guavas and mangoes. I was quite notorious in our neighbourhood. I walked around with a stick in my hand, hitting everyone. I bullied everyone. *[both laugh]*

If we happened to see a film, we would come home and re-enact scenes from it. Along with our friends, we sisters staged plays that I wrote. These plays were heroine-oriented stories. My role was of a fiery kind of heroine, and Asha who was very young, was made to play the king's daughter. Meena was the tough woman, a kind of vamp and the villain's accomplice. My cousin, Pandharinath [Padmini Kolhapure's father], whom we called 'Babu' played the villain.

We played *gilli-danda* and cards too. Baba fondly called me 'Tata Baba.' Whenever Mai complained to him about my bad behaviour, he used to tell her: 'I won't be here long. But this girl will look after you all.'

We were very naughty. Whenever Baba heard we had gone too far, he would make us stand in a line and stare at us. We'd burst out crying. He would then turn to me and ask: 'Do you know why I called you here?' In a meek tone, I answered: 'Yes, I know.' 'Good. Now go.'

That was all he needed to say. It was enough for us. He never used to hit us, but Mai often spanked us. She used to catch hold of me — she wore heavy gold bracelets, *paatli* and *gote,* the kind of bracelets Maharashtrians traditionally wear — and when I got the full weight of them on my back, I would run for cover! *[laughs]*

NMK: It sounds like you were a spirited child. Did you always manage to get away with everything?

LM: Almost. I must tell you an interesting story. In those days we had two-anna coins. There was a shop near our house in Sangli where we bought groceries. I was about five or six. One day my mother asked Vitthal, our young servant, to go and buy a bar of soap. The shopkeeper, Chilia, whom I knew, sent Vitthal back saying: 'The two-anna coin is fake.'

So snatching the coin from Vitthal, I said: 'I'll get the soap.' I ran straight to the shop and said: 'Chilia! Give me the soap!' He gave it to me at once. After all, my father was quite a celebrated man in the neighbourhood. 'Here's the money,' I said, quickly dropping the fake coin into his cashbox.

The teen-aged Mangeshkar sisters: seated are Lata (left) and cousin Malti (right). Behind them stand Meena (left) and Asha. Indore. Circa, *early 1940s.*

I ran home and boasted: 'Look! I have the soap.' My father asked how I had managed it. I went silent. Then Mai turned to me and said in a firm tone: 'Tell me how you brought the soap home. Tell me right now.' I answered sheepishly: 'I left the money there.' 'The fake coin?' 'Yes.' 'Very well, take this two-anna coin. Go back and apologise.'

Despite my copious tears Baba insisted, saying: 'You have no choice. Tell Chilia you gave him a counterfeit coin. Give him this money and apologise. You will have to learn.'

The young Mangeshkars: Usha (left), Lata, Meena and brother Hridaynath.

NMK: You had a most lively childhood but clearly one in which wholesome values were impressed on you. Today there is so much emphasis on material things, owning iPads and mobiles at a very young age. When did you own your first radio?

LM: In 1947. When I was eighteen, I managed to buy a radio. We were living in Nanachowk in those days and I remember I kept the radio safely aside till I could have a special moment to hear it for the first time. So one day when I was alone, I spread a *chhatai* on the floor and lay down. I switched the radio on and the first thing I heard was K.L. Saigal had died. It was the 18th of January 1947. I put the radio off, got up and rolled up the *chhatai*.

A few days later, I went back to the shop from where I had bought the radio and returned it.

NMK: What terrible news to hear, especially as you were such a great Saigal fan. If we may go back to the 1930s — what happened to your singing lessons during the time the family was facing financial problems? I believe your father had become virtually bankrupt.

LM: Baba produced three Marathi films through the Balwant Picture Company, a film company he set up with his theatre partners. The first of the three productions was *Krishna Arjun Yuddha*. [YouTube has a rare clip showing Deenanath Mangeshkar singing 'Suhasya tujhe manasi mohi' from the film]. But the films didn't do well and he lost a lot of money. In 1937, he closed his film company down — that was the year Hridaynath was born in Sangli. Baba then revived the Balwant Sangeet Mandali, his theatre company.

We went touring from here to there — Poona, Kolhapur, Satara, Goa, Miraj and other places. Travelling was exciting for us children.

I couldn't study singing for a long time because our financial problems didn't go away. Our lives completely changed then. In 1940, Baba had to close down the theatre company too. He ended up losing a lot of money and decided to cut off from the theatre world. My lessons did suffer but nature gave me a passion for singing that never left me.

NMK: How did your father manage then?

LM: We had so many debts. The family home in Sangli had to be auctioned. I am sure my parents felt the emotional pain of losing the old house but we were still children. In 1940, we moved to Poona and lived in rented accommodation. In 1941, our Sangli house was finally auctioned and we bought a place in Poona and settled there. The money we needed to run the house came from Baba's concerts in which I performed too.

Baba developed high blood pressure and his health was failing. Mai and we children were the only ones in the house. He was very ill and suffered severe nosebleeds. I was the only one who managed to stop him from doing things that worsened his condition as he used to listen to me.

One day when I was sitting near him, a friend dropped by and told us a man in the neighbourhood had died. Mai exclaimed: 'What a place this is! People are dying all around us. Only widows live here.' Baba said: 'Next Friday at 11.20, I will die.' I laughed and said: 'What are you saying?' 'Don't laugh. My time is over,' was Baba's reply. He knew a lot about astrology and even predicted his time of death. He repeated: 'My time has come. If I survive next Friday then I'll live till I'm eighty.' We made light of it and Meena and I went out to play.

On Thursday night Baba vomited blood. The next day, on 24th April, 1942, some friends took him to Sassoon Hospital in Poona. I did not realise he was seriously ill, so I didn't go with him. Just as Baba had predicted, he passed away at precisely 11.20. He was forty-two.

NMK: What was your first reaction when you heard the news?

LM: When Mai returned home from the hospital, she told me what had happened. The first thing I did was to lock Hridaynath and Usha in the kitchen. They were so young. I didn't want them to hear the news. Besides, Hridaynath was unwell too. I cried a little and then went completely silent. An hour later, I turned to Mai and asked: 'Where can I work? How do I earn money?' It was the only thought in my mind. During the time my father was unwell, I knew the responsibility of the family would fall on me. We cremated Baba in Poona and immersed his ashes in Nasik.

NMK: It's quite amazing that you had such a strong sense of responsibility, especially having been, as you say, a playful and mischievous child.

LM: After Baba died I had no choice. I had to work. I was responsible for running the house and was the eldest in our family of five young siblings: my sisters Meena, Asha and Usha and brother Hridaynath. He had serious health problems and had caught tuberculosis in a leg bone. The swelling had started when Baba was alive and a wound developed after he died. Hridaynath's leg has been affected since that time.

In the early 1940s, there wasn't much playback singing, so acting was the only option. Moreover, I couldn't have worked as a playback singer because my voice was thin. I was young. Only thirteen. But I did sing in the Marathi films in which I acted. I remember thinking: 'What kind of song is this? Why do I have to keep singing it over and over again? This is no song!' I believed songs should come from musical plays or have a classical base.

NMK: Your acting years began in 1942 and you subsequently worked in four Marathi films: *Pahili Mangalagaur, Chimukla Sansaar, Maaze Baal* and *Gajabhau*. The 1943 film *Gajabhau* was the Marathi film in which you sang your first Hindi song.

LM: Yes. The song was 'Hindustan ke logon ab to mujhko pehechano' and not 'Mata ek sapoot ki duniya badal de tu' as widely reported. Meenakshi sang 'Mata ek sapoot...' and I sang a few lines, a few words. Not the whole song.

NMK: In countless articles, 'Mata ek sapoot...' has, in fact, been named as your first Hindi song, albeit in a Marathi film. I hope your answer sets the record straight.

Coming back to your brief acting years, you then worked in four Hindi films: *Badi Maa*, *Jeevan Yatra*, *Subhadra* and *Mandir*. In your last Hindi/Marathi film *Chhatrapati Shivaji*, and years later in 2000, you appeared in *Pukar* in a song sequence. Did acting give you any pleasure?

LM: I had no other choice but to act in films. Before Baba died, an employee of his theatre company, Shripad Joshi, used to come to our house in Poona. One day, he took me to see the famous actor/director Master Vinayak, Nanda's father whose full name was Vinayak Damodar Karnataki. Mr. Joshi asked me to sing and Master Vinayak liked my voice. He offered me a job at Navyug Chitrapat Film Company in Poona.

My father didn't like the idea of me working in films and said he wouldn't allow it.

When Master Vinayak heard my father had passed away, he came to see us and once again offered me a job. I started working at Navyug within a month of Baba's demise. I had a three-month contract and played minor roles, earning around 300 rupees for the whole period.

Master Vinayak was casting for his film, *Pahili Mangalagaur,* and gave me a small role as the younger sister of the heroine, played by Snehprabha Pradhan. When the shooting was about to start, he had a disagreement with the studio and left. R.S. Junnarkar took over the film's direction. On 31st December, 1942, when my contract had ended, we moved to Kolhapur to join Master Vinayak. By that time, he had started his own film company, Prafulla Pictures, in Kolhapur. I was on the company payroll and was paid 60 rupees a month.

By 1947, my monthly salary was 200 rupees. I went to the studio everyday and spent the whole day working.

Meena, Usha and Asha also appeared in a song sequence in a 1943 Marathi film, *Maaze Baal*. My sisters didn't have proper roles but were in a scene in which a group of children are seen singing.

NMK: What was it like facing the camera for the first time?

LM: I never liked it — the make-up, the lights. People ordering you about, say this dialogue, say that dialogue. I felt so uncomfortable. A terrible thing happened to me on the first day of filming *Pahili Mangalagaur*. The director R.S. Junnarkar looked at me and said: 'Your eyebrows are too broad. Can we have them trimmed?' 'Chalega [sure],' I said meekly but a little shocked.

He then instructed the make-up man to trim my eyebrows. It was the look in the 1940s movies — thin eyebrows. They took me to the make-up room. I kept mum. If they had trimmed only my eyebrows, it might have been all right but the make-up man then cut back my hairline too. They said my forehead was too narrow. What could I say? So I answered in a resigned tone: 'Chalega.'

When the shooting was over, I returned home and that's when I started crying. *[laughs]* Mai asked me: 'What's wrong?' 'They cut my eyebrows and cut back my hairline. I didn't like it. I won't work there any more. This is terrible.' Mai consoled me

Lata Mangeshkar never enjoyed being in front of the camera, but circumstances forced her to find work in films.

saying: 'Don't feel bad. Your eyebrows and hair will grow back. Why are you crying?' I calmed down a little. But what upset me most was that I had to trim my hairline for months because of film continuity.

When I left Navyug and went to Kolhapur, I let my hairline grow back to its natural place. The only good thing about the whole story was my forehead looked a little broader. It was very narrow. *[smiles]*

In truth, I never liked acting. The day I started working as a playback singer, I prayed to God: 'No more acting in films.' He listened to me and I got a fairly good position in playback singing.

NMK: In which year did you move to Bombay?

LM: In 1945. Master Vinayak closed down his company in Kolhapur and started making films in Bombay. Everyone who was working for him, including my family, were housed in rooms in a large residence attached to the Shankar Sheth Shiv and Ram Temples in Nanachowk. The cameraman Papa Bulbule and his family lived on the floor above us.

The house is now completely destroyed — though the temples are still standing.

We were nine family members — Mai, my sisters, brother, cousin Indira and her two children. We had a large sitting room, a small bedroom and a veranda on the ground floor. We all slept in the small bedroom. We often put down a mattress on the floor and slept wherever we felt like. The veranda doubled up as 'the hall,' our main sitting area. We had a separate little kitchen and a bathing area. The toilets were situated in the common parts of the house and shared by everyone.

Before we settled in Nanachowk, Meena and I stayed for a short time with Master Vinayak and his family in Kumud Villa, their rented house on Grant Road. During that period, Mai, my sisters Asha, Usha and brother Hridaynath were living with my maternal grandmother in Thalner. And then the whole family was together again.

NMK: I believe Master Vinayak introduced you to Noorjehanji during the making of *Badi Maa* in which you had a small role too. Was she a kind of guru to you?

LM: No. Noorjehanji was not my guru and I wasn't her disciple. But I liked her singing very much. Before I started working in films, I had seen *Khandaan* in which she starred opposite Pran who was the hero of the movie. During my time at Prafulla Pictures in Kolhapur, I was given a small role in *Badi Maa,* a Hindi film that Master Vinayak was directing with Noorjehanji, Sitara Devi and Yakub. I sang the song 'Maata tere charno

The outside world may have set them up as rivals, but in reality, Noorjehan and Lata Mangeshkar shared a warm and affectionate friendship for over 50 years. They are seen here at a party held at St James Court Hotel, London. Early 1990s.

mein,' on and off screen. People mistakenly say the song was picturised on Asha but it isn't the case. The other song in the film 'Tum maa ho badi maa,' was sung by Meenakshi and I sang a few lines too.

The first schedule of *Badi Maa* took place in Kolhapur and Noorjehanji came to film a song. They converted the studio's music room into a living area and Noorjehanji, her husband, Shaukat Hussain Rizvi Sahib and their six-month old son, Akbar, stayed there.

One day, I was on the *Badi Maa* set and Master Vinayak introduced us saying: 'This is Noorjehanji. Sing her a song.' So I sang Raag Jaijaiwanti. She then asked me to sing a film song, so I sang R.C. Boral's 'Jeevan hai bekaar bina tumhaare' from the film *Wapas*.

While I was singing I remembered Baba's words: 'If you sing in front of your guru, consider yourself a guru.' So I sang with that thought in mind and she liked my voice. She told me to practise and said I will be a very good singer some day. We met again in Bombay during the completion of *Badi Maa*.

Noorjehanji migrated to Pakistan in 1947 but she called me often from Karachi and I phoned her too. She used to ask me to sing 'Dheere se aaja ri akhiyan mein,' the lullaby from *Albela* or some other song. It created quite a stir in Bombay and people were commenting: 'These two keep phoning each other and singing.' So all the telephone operators started eavesdropping on our calls. *[both laugh].*

NMK: Did you both meet again?

LM: We arranged to meet once in the early '50s at Wagah, at the Indo-Pak border. I made my way there with my sisters Meena, Usha and a friend, Mangala. And Noorjehanji arrived with a huge pot of *biryani!* We all ate together and had a wonderful time.

Almost every year, during May and June, she visited London with her family. I was often there at the same time and we would meet. She cooked me lavish meals and always greeted me with much affection. I called her 'Apa' [elder sister].

In 1982, Noorjehanji came to Bombay to attend a big musical event and Dilip Kumar and I welcomed her. In later years, when I heard she was unwell, I called her a few times in Karachi. Her kidneys were in a bad state. She was on dialysis and spoke of her suffering and pain. On 23rd December, 2000, I was in Kolhapur when my nephew, Baijnath, called to say Noorjehanji had passed away. I was very sad.

NMK: Your friendship lasted fifty-five years from the first time you met on the sets of *Badi Maa*. Coming back to the '40s, you were still in your teens and working in films. What became of your musical training?

LM: I stopped studying classical music after Baba died. I practised on my own but didn't have any formal training at that time. It was Master Vinayak who said I must further the lessons Baba had given me. He called Ustaad Aman Ali Khan Bhendibazaarwale and at an initiation ceremony held at Kumud Villa on 11th August, 1945, a *gandha* was tied and I became his disciple.

The first *raag* he taught me was Hamsadhwani. It is an evening *raag* and still my favourite. Many years later, Salil Chowdhury based the duet 'Jaa tose nahin boloon kanhaiyya,' on the same *raag*. I sang this duet with Manna Dey for *Parivar*.

Aman Ali Khan Sahib was a good and kind man and loved me like his own daughter. He gave me singing lessons at Master Vinayak's house in Shivaji Park. The moment he arrived, he first closed the door behind him and made me eat an omelette rolled in a *roti.* He brought me an omelette and a *roti* everyday because he thought I was too thin and insisted I eat before we start.

The lessons lasted about two hours. A harmonium and *tabla* player accompanied me as I played the *tanpura* and sang.

To this day I can't say I have ever stopped missing my father, but when I began singing again with Khan Sahib, I remember feeling Baba's absence deeply. Khan Sahib taught me for some time and then left for Talegaon. I waited for him to return, but he didn't. We had no news of him. A few months later Master Vinayak found me another teacher, Amanat Khan Devaswale, who was the nephew of the famous singer Rajjab Ali Khan.

He taught many film people, including Nargisji. Her mother, Jaddanbai, was keen she learn how to sing. But Khan Sahib soon discovered Nargisji much preferred playing tennis to practising the scales! He was a wonderful teacher and a great singer but unfortunately our lessons lasted a short while because he left for Indore and there, very suddenly, he passed away.

In the 1970s, I learned singing with Tulsidas Sharma, a disciple of Bade Ghulam Ali Khan Sahib. I had no free time but wanted to continue studying. Then Sharmaji passed away. And again my musical training stopped. But singing in films was practice too, and I was singing from morning to night.

NMK: Master Vinayak was of the same family as V. Shantaram. How long did you work with him?

LM: Until 1947. I acted in minor roles in a few of Master Vinayak's films, but as I told you, I never liked acting. On 19th August, 1947, Master Vinayak died. It was a big shock to us. The last film he had started was *Mandir* which was completed by director Dinkar Patil.

Soon after Master Vinayak had died, his manager came to where Prafulla Pictures housed us in Nanachowk and said: 'You'll have to move out now. The company has closed down.' We didn't know what to do and found ourselves in the same difficult situation we faced in 1942 — with no money and many mouths to feed. Although I had worked continuously, I wasn't paid for over six months because Master Vinayak's film company had fallen on bad times.

Our neighbour, the cameraman Papa Bulbule, who also worked at Prafulla Pictures said to me: 'I know a music director who needs a new singer. If you want to sing, then come with me.'

He took me to Central Studio in Tardeo to meet Harishchandra Bali. I sang a song which he liked very much. He knew my father too.

While I was recording Harishchandra Bali's song for *Love is Blind*, a film that was finally shelved, a Pathan, a film extra supplier appeared and said: 'Come tomorrow to Filmistan studio in Goregaon. Master Ghulam Haider has called you.' I replied: 'But I don't know him. What will I do there?' He said: 'Just come.'

Getting ready to record a song for Yash Chopra's Lamhe *at HMV Studios, Flora Fountain, Bombay. 1991. Photo credit: Peter Chappell.*

Top: Pahili Mangalagaur *(1942), was the first film in which Lata Mangeshkar appeared (aged thirteen). Above: Rare still from* Gajabhau *(1943). Lata Mangeshkar (left) sang her first Hindi song in this Marathi film.*

Top: In the Hindi film Jeevan Yatra *(1946). Above: Still from Master Vinayak's mythological film* Subhadra *(1946), starring Shanta Apte (left) and Lata Mangeshkar. The film had music composed by Vasant Desai.*

Wearing a saree is Indore cousin Malti, flanked by Asha (to her right) and Meena. Lata Mangeshkar has always worn anklets. Here she is five or six years old.

From 1945 to 1952, Lata Mangeshkar and her family lived in two rooms in Nanachowk, Bombay. It was from this house that she travelled to the studios everyday, sometimes recording six songs a day.

Inset: With Geeta Dutt rehearsing a verse of the same song as Raj Kapoor looks on. Famous, Tardeo. 1959.

Lata Mangeshkar, Mahendra Kapoor (left of LM), Manna Dey, Raj Kapoor and Mukesh (top right) rehearsing the Jis Desh Mein Ganga Behti Hai (1960) *song 'Hai aag hamaare seene mein.' Chorus singers are seen in the background.*

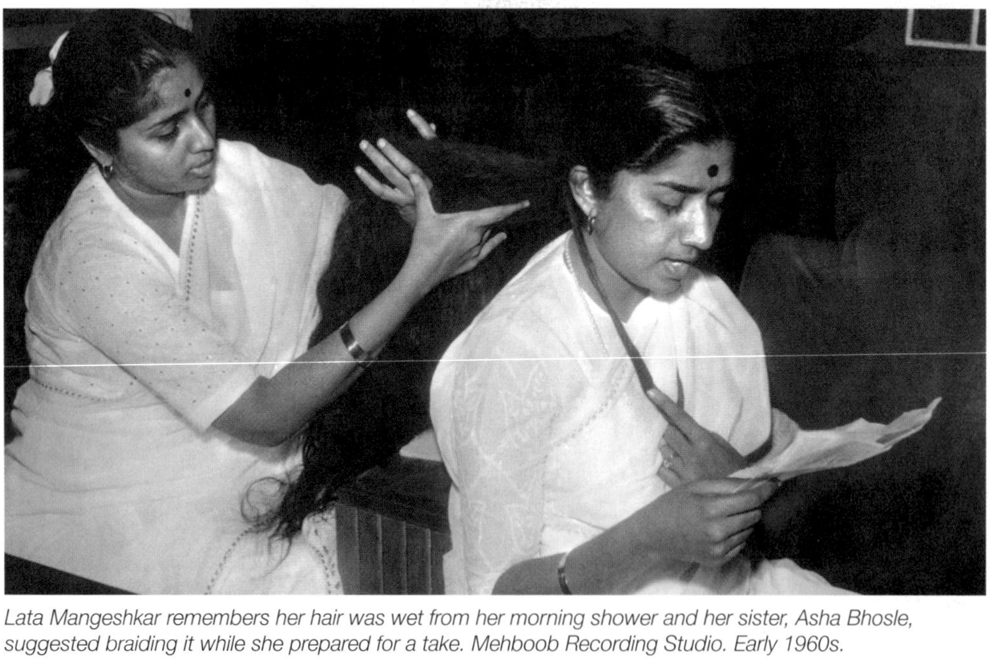

Lata Mangeshkar remembers her hair was wet from her morning shower and her sister, Asha Bhosle, suggested braiding it while she prepared for a take. Mehboob Recording Studio. Early 1960s.

Mukesh was a close friend who shared a common love for singing star K.L. Saigal. Saigal's harmonium was one of Mukesh's prized possessions.

Lata Mangeshkar was a great fan of M.S. Subbulakshmi. They are the only female singers to have been conferred the Bharat Ratna, India's highest civilian honour.

Left to right: Talat Mahmood, Mukesh, Lata Mangeshkar, Mohammed Rafi and Manna Dey. These extraordinarily talented singers (and Kishore Kumar) gave India its popular music through Hindi cinema.

Flanked by sisters Meena Khadikar (right of LM) and Usha Mangeshkar. Meena's children, Rachana and Yogesh sit on either side of their grandmother, Shudhhamati Mangeshkar.

With Jaikishan on double bass, and Shankar on piano. Lata Mangeshkar believes few composers had the range of this most famous duo. Circa *1960s.*

NMK: Master Ghulam Haider is credited for introducing the Lahore school of music and the *dholak* in the film song. Were you already familiar with his music before you had met him?

LM: Yes. I had a lot of respect for him. I'll have to go back in time and tell you a story. In 1941, when my father was alive, *Khazanchi* was released. It had music by Master Ghulam Haider and lyrics by Wali Sahib. Master Ghulam Haider even sang a duet in the film, 'Saawan ke nazaare hain,' with Shamshad Begum. *Khazanchi* was a big hit everywhere and in Poona too. So, a competition was organised and the top prize was for the best singer who could sing two *Khazanchi* songs. So I did it again! When my father went to Bombay, I sneaked off and added my name to the list. About 114 girls signed up for the contest. When Baba returned and heard what I had done, he was annoyed with me. But this time he said: 'If you don't win the first prize, I'll be put to shame.'

In my childhood I had this thing about being Master Deenanath's daughter. In other words, I considered myself a really important person — the daughter of such an eminent father. I always had this feeling in my head.

The contest began and all the girls were called onto the stage. Each girl was asked to start by saying her name. When it came to my turn, I stood up and shouted loudly: 'Lata Deenanath Mangeshkar!' *[both laugh]* Everyone clapped because Baba was famous in Maharashtra. I sang 'Laut gayi paapan andhiyaari' and 'Nainon ke baan ki reet anokhi,' originally sung by Shamshad Begum in *Khazanchi*. I went home and later heard I had won the first prize — a *dilruba*.

So with this memory in mind, I went to meet Ghulam Haider Sahib. He asked me to sing and I sang one of his compositions, 'Main to orun gulaabi chunariya aaj re,' from Mehboob Khan's *Humayun.* Then I sang Noorjehanji's 'Bulbulo mat ro yahan' from *Zeenat*. I was so nervous I sang the song out of tune. Ghulam Haider Sahib asked me: 'Have you had singing lessons?' 'Yes. Amanat Khan Devaswale was my teacher.' He knew my guru personally and said: 'I see! You were taught by Khan Sahib and you can't sing in tune?' *[laughs]*

NMK: It must have been a harrowing experience!

LM: I couldn't tell him how terrified I was. But he liked my singing and called me back two days later. As he was busy recording, I sat outside the whole day with nothing to eat or drink. At 5 in the evening, he called me into the recording studio and said: 'I want you to sing the heroine's songs in *Shaheed*.'

But the film's producer, Shashadhar Mukherjee, wasn't keen and said: 'Lata's voice isn't the right voice for Kamini Kaushal. It's too thin and won't sound good.' Masterji was irritated and said: 'All right. You'll sing in *Majboor*, a Bombay Talkies film I am working on. Come with me.' And off we went to Goregaon station. We had to wait on the platform for the train to arrive. Masterji was standing near me, holding a 555 cigarette tin in his hand. He started tapping a beat on the cigarette tin and turned to me: 'Sing this song, Lata.' He sang 'Dil mera toda mujhe kahin ka na chhoda haaye tere pyaar ne' and I sang after him. He exclaimed: 'Yes! That's it! That's how I want you to sing it.' The train arrived and we went to Bombay Talkies in Malad.

We rehearsed 'Dil mera toda' and just two days later the song was recorded.

During the recording of *Majboor*'s duet 'Ab darne ki koi baat nahin angrezi chhora chala gaya woh gora gora chala gaya' [There's nothing more to fear, the British lad has gone, the white boy has gone] I met Mukesh Bhaiya for the first time. It is possible the song words were a light-hearted reference to the British leaving India in 1947!

I knew singing for Ghulam Haider Sahib was a huge break for me, and as a result other music directors asked me to sing for them, including Khemchand Prakash and Anil Biswas. Khemchand Prakashji was very fond of me and I called him 'Chachaji' [Uncle].

NMK: When did you meet the other playback singers?

LM: I met Kishore Kumar around the time that I was working with Khemchand Prakashji. I used to travel by train from Grant Road to Malad. One day, Kishoreda got on at Mahalaxmi, the stop after Grant Road, and sat in my compartment. I thought he looked very familiar and wondered who he was. He was wearing a *kurta-pyjama* with a scarf tied round his neck, and was holding a cane in his hand. We both got off at Malad. Bombay Talkies studio was a long way from the station and sometimes I walked or took a *taanga*. That day I decided to hire a *taanga* and Kishoreda hired one too. I set off and so did he. We finally entered the studio and I saw his *taanga* right behind me. I thought to myself: 'Something strange going on. This fellow is following me.' So I went straight into the recording studio where Khemchandji was sitting, and under my breath, I asked: 'Uncle, who is this boy? He's been following me.'

He looked up to see Kishoreda. Khemchandji laughed and said: 'He's Kishore. Ashok Kumar's brother.'

We were introduced to one another and that day we recorded our first duet 'Ye kaun aaya re karke solah singar' for *Ziddi.* In fact, *Ziddi* was Kishoreda's first film as playback singer.

Lata Mangeshkar's song 'Aayega aanewala' created a storm throughout India and instantly won her an army of fans. Palace Theatre, Kolhapur. Early 1950s.

NMK: This film is also famous for making a star of Dev Anand. And Dev Sahib always talks about how proud he was that Kishore Kumar became his singing voice in so many films. What about Khemchand Prakash's most famous song in *Mahal* with lyrics by Nakshab Jaaravchi — 'Aayega aanewala?' What do you remember about the song?

LM: When Khemchand Prakashji composed 'Aayega aanewala,' some people at Bombay Talkies liked it and others didn't. The *asthayi* was initially composed in two versions. Khemchandji believed in the song and knew it was good and would be popular. But the producers, Savak Vacha and Ashok Kumarji, had different opinions. Ashok Kumarji said: 'It's good,' while Mr. Vacha said: 'No, it isn't.'

It was an amazing experience. We spent the whole day in the recording studio working on 'Aayega aanewala.' *Mahal*'s director, Kamal Amrohi Sahib, clearly understood how, through the song, he could make the scene full of mood and atmosphere.

NMK: To remind those who haven't seen this 1949 classic — in this scene, the hero [Ashok Kumar] takes shelter from a storm and enters an old dilapidated house. He finds a portrait of a bearded man who happens to be his spitting image. The hero is puzzled as he has never entered this old house before nor knows the man in the painting. The atmosphere is eerie with swinging chandeliers and long shadows falling across the walls. The clock strikes two. A brief moment of silence follows and a song is heard: 'Khamosh hai zamaanaa...' So little happens on the surface and yet we know the hero's life will never be the same again. It's a stunning cinematic moment. How did you make 'Aayega aanewala' work so well in the film?

LM: We decided to make the song sound as though it were coming from a great distance, to create an effect like that. I stood in a corner of the studio and the microphone was placed in the middle of the room. Singing the first verse: 'Khaamosh hai zamaanaa...' I walked slowly towards the mike, and when I was close to it, I sang the main refrain, 'Aayega aayega aanewala.' We repeated this process many times and finally the song was recorded. It started with these introductory lines:

Khaamosh hai zamaanaa chup chaap hain sitaare
Aaram se hai duniya bekal hai dil ke maare
Aise mein koi aahat is tarah aa rahi hai
Jaise ke chal raha ho mann mein koi hamaare
Ya dil dhadak raha hai is aas ke sahaare

Time stands still. The stars are silent
The world is at rest. Yet my heart is uneasy
Suddenly I hear footsteps approaching
As though someone were walking through my heart
Or is it the sound of my heart quickening with hope?

Aayega aayega aayega
Aayega aanewala aayega
Aayega aayega...

The one who is meant to return will come back

NMK: In today's technology it's so easy to create all kinds of sound effects, but in the late 1940s, the idea of achieving sound perspective in the way you did is ingenious. The *Mahal* song really sounds otherworldly. Do you remember anything else about that day?

LM: Nargisji happened to be in the studio in a nearby room. Her mother, the celebrated singer, Jaddanbai, was with her that day. When I finished recording, I went out. Jaddanbai called me to her and asked: 'What is your name?' 'Lata Mangeshkar.' 'I see. Are you Maharashtrian?' 'Yes.' 'Your Urdu is very good.' 'I'm trying.' 'You pronounce the word "baghair" very well.' That's how I met Nargisji and her mother.

NMK: Did everyone accept the song once it was recorded?

LM: No. There was still a lot of discussion about whether we should re-do it or replace it as producer Savak Vacha remained unconvinced. When the film was released, it was the first of *Mahal*'s songs to become popular. By that time, Khemchandji was in hospital. He passed away not knowing what a success it was. I felt terrible because he never knew how famous he had become.

The very same thing happened to Ghulam Mohammed Sahib. He composed music for a few small films, but it was only after he died that his music became all the rage on *Pakeezah*'s release.

Kamal Amrohi Sahib who chose to work with Ghulam Mohammed Sahib in *Pakeezah* was an excellent writer and lyricist too. Whenever he made a film, he worked closely with the songwriter and got precisely the kind of lyrics he wanted. Almost suggesting the words and mood.

You can hear strains of Rajasthani folk music in *Pakeezah* because Ghulam Mohammed Sahib was from Bikaner. For example, 'Thade rahiyo' is completely Rajasthani and shows the composer's own background. He worked for many years as Naushad Sahib's assistant and was an excellent *tabla* player, and played both the *tabla* and *dholak* in many of Naushad Sahib's compositions. He had two brothers: Abdul Karim who was a good *tabla* player too, and Ibrahim who played the harmonium and sang. In fact, we shared the same guru, Amanat Khan Devaswale, and during the time when we were studying music, Ibrahim often came to our house. When Ghulam Mohammed Sahib became a music director in his own right, Ibrahim then worked as Naushad Sahib's assistant.

NMK: There are some extraordinary songs in *Pakeezah*, including 'Inhin logon ne' written by Majrooh Sultanpuri and 'Chalte chalte' by Kaifi Azmi. Did you ever visit the *Pakeezah* set to watch the shooting?

LM: No. I wasn't keen on visiting film sets. I had my fill when I was acting in Marathi films. The endless takes, the hot lights. None of it appealed to me. I didn't like acting, so never thought it was particularly interesting to watch a film shoot.

NMK: The only duet in *Pakeezah* is the beautiful 'Chalo dildaar chalo' by Kaifi Azmi which is still so popular. Can you tell me when you met Mohammed Rafi?

LM: In 1947. I don't remember which song we had to rehearse, or for which film, but he came to the rehearsal room somewhere close to where I lived in Nanachowk. It was the first time I met him. Before meeting him, however, I had seen him in *Jugnu.* He appears in a scene singing a refrain of the song 'Woh apne yaad dilaane ko.'

I had this habit — especially when singing with Rafi Sahib — of working out in my mind a *taan* and at a particular point, and only during the take, did I sing it. Taken aback, Rafi Sahib would say: 'I see! That was unexpected!' I teased him a little but we worked well together.

NMK: You said the first duet you sang with Mukeshji was 'Angrezi chhora chala gaya' in *Majboor*. How was your relationship with him?

LM: We shared a lot of love and respect and looked out for one another — especially if either of us made a mistake. Sometimes a singer can make a mistake or forget a song word. We reassured each other by saying: 'Never mind, it will be all right.'

Mukesh Bhaiya had this habit of clearing his throat in the middle of singing. I used to pull his leg: 'What, Mukesh Bhaiya? Why do you keep doing that?' And the poor fellow hurriedly said: 'Sorry, Didi. I won't do it again.' I smiled and told him I was only joking.

Sometimes when we were recording and a musician played a solo piece slightly off key, Mukesh Bhaiya would turn to me and say: 'Who is copying me?' *[both laugh]*

There was a lot of affection between us. I would visit his house and spend time with his family and his three children, Nitin, Rita and Neelu. When Nitin was very young, he sometimes accompanied his father to the recordings.

NMK: Did you help each other find work?

LM: It was Mukesh Bhaiya who introduced me to Naushad Ali. One day he came to Nanachowk and said: 'Didi, come with me. I want to take you to Naushad Sahib because he wants you to sing for him.' I recorded some songs for composer Shyam Sundar's film *Lahore* and I believe Naushad Sahib had heard them.

I was singing for a number of film composers by the late '40s. When I would meet a composer with whom I hadn't previously worked, he would invariably ask me to sing. The one thing I disliked was auditioning. I had sung at so many classical music concerts with my father and somehow felt auditioning was humiliating. So, from the outset I told Mukesh Bhaiya: 'I won't audition for Naushad Sahib or any other composer. If they want me, then I will record the song.' Mukesh Bhaiya replied: 'All right. Let's at least go and talk to him.'

We went to Kardar Studio and met Naushad Sahib. Ghulam Mohammed Sahib was working as his assistant then and he was there too. Perhaps Mukesh Bhaiya had already warned them I disliked auditioning. When I was introduced to Naushad Sahib, he cleverly said: 'Latabai, I have heard you mentioned many times. I hear you sing very well. I'd like to hear you but don't think you're on trial. Nothing of the sort. But why not sing a *ghazal?'* So I sang 'Umeed ke rangeen jhoole mein ek aas bandhaaye jaati hai' from *Lahore*. It didn't take me long to figure out Naushad Sahib just wanted to hear my Urdu pronunciation because he was going to ask me to sing for *Andaaz*. He heard me sing the *ghazal* and was pleased.

The first song I sang for him was a duet with G.M. Durrani, 'Haye chhore ki jaat badi bewafa' for *Chandni Raat*. Durrani Sahib made a personal comment I didn't like, about a necklace I was wearing and I mentioned this exchange to Naushad Sahib. He understood I was a sensitive person and didn't want my feelings hurt. So he asked a young singer, Sadat Khan, to record another *Chandni Raat* duet with me — but this was edited out of the film. I believe a disc of the duet existed.

NMK: How were your working conditions?

LM: I worked hard, recording songs from morning to night. Running from one studio to another. I never felt like doing anything else. I ended up going hungry all day because I didn't even know recording studios had canteens and I could buy something to eat or get some tea. I often went without food and water for the whole day. If someone happened to mention there was a canteen in the studio, then I'd eat something. The only thought that preoccupied me was how to look after my family. Somehow.

NMK: By the early 1950s, you were singing in many films. Did anything improve on the money front?

LM: *[smiles]* I can't say my financial situation was good, but neither was it bad, because I had a lot of work. We decided to stay on in the same two rooms in Nanachowk where Prafulla Pictures first housed us. I started paying rent there.

Between 1952 and 1960, we lived in a three-bedroom flat in Walkeshwar which we managed to buy. It was the first time I had a room of my own. We sold the Walkeshwar flat in 1960 and bought a first floor flat in Prabhu Kunj on Peddar Road. We have lived here ever since.

I used to give Mai all the money I earned. She ran the household and saved whatever she could. Despite the heavy workload, we weren't always paid on time. Some producers held on to the money. Very often I wasn't paid at all. We singers then decided we should be paid on the spot. In truth, money did not matter to me that much because the songs we sang in those days gave me so much pleasure.

The greats of Hindi film music: (left to right) Saraswati Devi (India's early female film composer), Lata Mangeshkar, Madan Mohan, Jaikishan, Anil Biswas and Naushad Ali at a meeting of the Music Directors' Association.

In 1948, I was working on *Mahal*, *Barsaat, Andaaz*, *Dulari*, *Badi Bahen* and *Girls' School,* a film whose music was composed by Anil Biswas — these films were released in 1949. So there was a lot of work and it was going well. I recorded two songs in the morning, two in the afternoon, two in the evening and two at night. I left home in the morning and got back at 3 am the next day and that's when I ate. After a few hours sleep, I would wake up at six, get dressed, catch the train and travel from one recording studio to another. We were young, so we could work that hard. Perhaps today it isn't possible.

NMK: If you were recording so many songs in a day, how did you manage to learn them so quickly?

LM: In those days, most music directors called us to their music rooms or to a hired hall where we rehearsed the song two or three times prior to the recording session. So, on any given day, we were ready to record, say two songs by Naushad Sahib or Anil Biswas. But the songs were always rehearsed in advance.

NMK: Were playback singers given any special status in those days?

LM: No! No importance at all was given to playback singers. Producers would think: 'Let them record, pay them and they can go.' End of story. I don't know if you've seen the 78 record of 'Aayega aanewala.' Well, the singer's name on the label is 'Kamini.' It was Madhubala's screen name in *Mahal.* I did get upset that our names never featured anywhere. I had to fight for it to happen and kept asking producers: 'Why don't you credit us?' The first time our names appeared on the screen and on disc was in *Barsaat* in 1949. It coincided with credit given to us in other films that year, including *Andaaz* and *Badi Bahen*.

'Aayega aanewala' became so popular that the radio station received thousands of request letters. People wrote in asking: 'Who is singing this song? We want to know her name.' So HMV was called

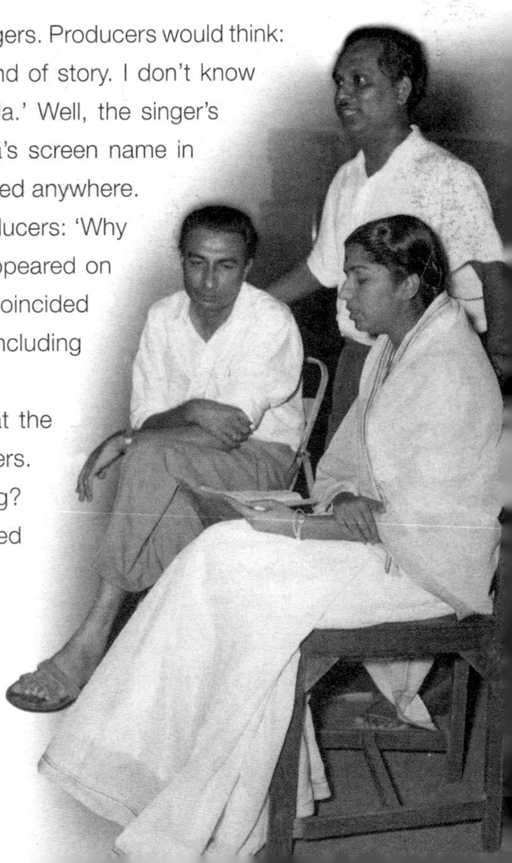

With Anil Biswas (standing) and Urdu poet/lyricist Sahir Ludhianvi who wrote many wonderful songs for Hindi cinema.

Anil Biswas was among the leading composers of the 1940s and '50s. Lata Mangeshkar met many film personalities at his home.

and asked to name the singer. Finally it was even announced on the radio: 'This song is sung by Lata Mangeshkar.' *[smiles]*

NMK: Interesting how you had to fight to become 'visible.' Gulzar Sahib once said that it was Sahir Ludhianvi who insisted that the names of the lyricists be announced on All India Radio alongside the names of the composers .

I am curious to know what the recording studios were like in the 1940s and 1950s.

LM: There weren't many in those days. Famous and Central were in Tardeo, and there was another studio also called Famous which was in Mahalakshmi. These studios had small halls used for recording. Filmistan in Goregoan had a small recording studio too, but on many occasions, we were obliged to record on the studio floor. Even the songs of Filmistan's own productions, *Nagin* and *Anarkali,* which were hugely successful films, were recorded on a studio stage.

When the day's shooting finished and everyone had left, we went onto the studio floor and recorded through the night. The place was full of dust, the lights were still burning hot and it was sweltering. We couldn't use the fans because of the noise they made. I have recorded so many songs in difficult and trying conditions.

NMK: I believe Mehboob Khan imported the latest German recording equipment. When did he open his recording studio?

LM: In 1956. He built a large recording studio within Mehboob Studio in Bandra. Naushad Sahib, Roshanji and S.D. Burman often worked there, and in later years, it was Laxmikant-Pyarelal's favourite studio. Before Mehboob Studio existed, Mehboob Sahib rented offices at Central Studio in Tardeo.

We had some excellent sound recordists: Minoo Katrak was working at Famous in Tardeo; Kaushik Baba was at Mehboob's and B.N. Sharma worked at Bombay Laboratories, known as Bombay Labs. Bombay Labs was in Dadar. Kaushik Baba later moved to Film Centre in Tardeo. They worked with whatever equipment was available in India in those days. Minoo Katrak recorded nearly all of Raj Kapoor's music at Famous because Raj Sahib liked working there. Sadly, Minoo Katrak fell ill and so his assistant, Bhansali, took over.

I remember an incident that took place in 1966 at Famous in Tardeo, while I was recording the *Mera Saaya* song, 'Nainon mein badara chhaaye' by Madan Mohanji. You know when musicians get tired, they start talking to one another and aren't attentive. So they weren't playing well and Madan Bhaiya was sitting in a corner. He was furious and shouted loudly. He got up to cross the room and by accident his fist went through the glass door. The glass shattered, leaving his hand dripping with blood. Then we made him sit down and calmed him down. He was so upset.

NMK: Famous in Tardeo opened in 1941 and was owned by Rajkumar Seksaria. Madan Mohan's son, Sanjeev Kohli, informed me it closed down in the late 1980s because smaller studios were in great vogue with their modern equipment and soon electronic recording replaced acoustic recording. This was also the time when all film production moved to Bombay's suburbs and Tardeo was considered too far. Which other composers worked at Famous during its heyday?

LM: Many did. Anil Biswas, Vasant Desai, and Shankar-Jaikishan. It was their favourite studio and many of their songs were recorded there. In the beginning, Laxmikant-Pyarelal worked there too. People would say: 'We must record in the same studio as Shankar-Jaikishan then our songs will be hits!' Even in the 1990s, music directors recorded the first song of a film there and then went elsewhere. The greatest hits were recorded at Famous in Tardeo. It was a very lucky studio.

NMK: I believe when you worked in shifts, one music director finished his session and another would arrive. Were they secretive about their tunes, not wanting the others to listen in?

LM: Some were hesitant to let anyone hear their tunes but most weren't. In fact, you won't believe it, but it was Naushad Sahib who recorded Roshanji's song 'Saari saari raat teri yaad sataaye' for *Aji Bas Shukriya*. We were at Mehboob Studios and Naushad Sahib arrived. He was such a respected composer and Roshanji had so much regard for him. Roshanji asked Naushad Sahib: 'Why don't you record my song for me today? It will make me happy.' So Naushad Sahib instructed me while I was singing. Of course he didn't change even a single note of Roshanji's original composition.

One day we happened to be at Filmistan and C. Ramchandra was working on the sad version of the *Anarkali* song 'Ye zindagi usi ki hai.' Roshanji was there too and when C. Ramchandra came to write music for the verse: 'Sunayegi ye daastaan shama mere mazaar ki,' he thought he didn't have the right tune for the verse. So he asked Roshanji to give it a go. Roshanji took the harmonium and composed the music for the lines:

Sunayegi ye daastan shama mere mazaar ki
Sunayegi ye daastan shama mere mazaar ki
Khizan mein bhi khil rehi ye kali anaar ki
Ise mazaar mat kaho
Ise mazaar mat kaho
Ye mahal hai pyaar ka
Ye zindagi usi ki hai...

The lamp that burns at my grave will tell my story
Even in autumn, this flower will blossom
Do not consider this a grave
This is a palace of love
My life belongs to you...

The rest of the song was of course C. Ramchandra's. The composers in those days held each other in such high esteem that these kinds of situations were not unusual.

NMK: How wonderful it must have been to be with creative people who thought the end result was more important than ego. You've spent so much of your life in those recording studios. Famous in Tardeo, for example, must be a treasure chest of memories for you.

LM: I have spent endless hours there. In the early days, there was no air-conditioning or any sort of comfort to make the work easier. Sometimes we started at 9 in the morning and returned home the next day. We were exhausted but were so happy working together. We were like one family — like brothers and sisters. I liked that.

One day, Anil Biswasji was recording a song for *Pardesi*. And just as we had entered the studio, it started raining. The Bombay monsoons can really be dreadful. It rained heavily that day and our cars were soon under some feet of water. We had no way of leaving the studio. We finished the song and then sent for something to eat. The next morning, when the rains stopped, we managed to get home.

Whenever I happened to visit the studio in Tardeo, the recording engineers Bhansali and Raman would greet me so warmly. I enjoyed working there. There was no board outside the building to identify the studio but everyone knew the place. Amazing things happened there too. Sometimes I'd get a letter from a fan saying: 'You were recording the other day and we were passing through Tardeo. We heard you were inside, so we came in and heard your song — we liked it very much.' *[laughs]*

NMK: That's the wonderful thing about working in Indian films: your fans are never far away! I can't imagine this happening in the West — the idea of a fan just strolling into a studio where Madonna is recording! Can you tell me how you went about recording a duet?

LM: In the early days both singers used the same microphone. I would stand facing the mike and the other artist would stand near me, leaving a little space between us. I had a big problem when singing with Hemant Kumar. Because he was much taller than me, I needed to use a small box or stool to stand on and sing. *[both laugh]*

NMK: Until magnetic recorders and magnetic tape came to India, I believe songs were recorded on wax discs. What were the technical difficulties that you faced?

LM: Earlier, we had to record the songs as 'live.' So, if any singer or musician made a mistake at any point of the recording we would have to start again from the top. We would end up with 20 or 30 takes and the next day, the music director would check them. Many times I was sent a message saying the song had to be re-recorded. It happened a lot, as the technical quality wasn't very good.

Also, we had to record two versions of a song: a four-minute version for the film, and a shorter version for HMV which was recorded at their studios. The HMV recording was used for the 78rpm disc, and because 78s could hold only three minutes and twenty seconds, you will find the disc version of the song often has a refrain less or verse repetitions have been edited out. So, the 78s are slightly different from the film version of the song.

Other interesting things happened. *Anokha Pyaar,* for instance, had two heroines. Nargisji played one heroine and Nalini Jaywant played the other. Anilda [Anil Biswas], who was composing the music for the film, decided that Meena Kapoor would sing for Nargisji and I will give playback for Nalini Jaywant. So in the film, Meena Kapoor sings the *ghazal* 'Mere liye woh gham-e-intezaar chhod gaye' for Nargisji, but when the time came for Meena Kapoor to record the HMV version, she was unwell. So, I ended up recording the *ghazal* and the disc version, when released, both versions were credited to me.

NMK: The history of recording is fascinating. I recently read Columbia Records first released the LP in 1948 in America, which revolutionised the music business because it played for 22 minutes on each side. Experts at *Saregama* informed me that the production of 78s ended in 1971. They also said the first LP of a Hindi film soundtrack was of *Mother India* [produced by HMV, India, 1958]. Then came the EP [45 rpm]. By the end of the 1960s, there were three formats: 78, 33⅓ and 45 rpm discs.

LM: In fact, I was under contract for a while with Columbia Records, India and have sung many non-film songs for them. I can still remember the blue labels on their 78 discs!

If I am not mistaken, I think magnetic recorders were imported into India by the early 1950s. I was not aware of the technical aspects of recording; we sang the songs and weren't qualified sound engineers. But when we started recording on tape, it meant the music director could immediately rewind the tape and check whether the song was well recorded or not. I believe the *Baiju Bawra* songs featured in the film were among the first to be recorded on magnetic tape. But the disc versions were recorded as 'live.'

I remember when I was recording the duet 'Tu ganga ki mauj main' at HMV Studios, I had a high temperature — 102. I fainted at the end of the recording.

NMK: Your voice doesn't have a trace of your being unwell. By the late '40s — and thanks to the high quality of playback singers like yourself and your colleagues — singing was no longer a defining talent, and as a result the doors opened to a new generation of actors in Hindi cinema. From the early 1950s, we see a greater sophistication and a more imaginative approach in the way songs were filmed. I am thinking of Raj Kapoor's brilliant dream sequence in *Awaara*. French dancer Madame Simkie choreographed this nine-minute sequence, and her work with Uday Shankar shows his influence in the choreography. Do you remember anything about the recording of 'Ghar aya mera pardesi'?

LM: We spent the whole day and night at Famous in Tardeo, working on the three-part song. I think there were a hundred musicians there. I sang the first and third part of the song: 'Tere bina aag ye chandni' and 'Ghar aya mera pardesi.' Manna Dey sang the middle section 'Ye nahin hai zindagi.' We didn't stop till the whole song was done. Once it was recorded, I recall we sat on the steps of Famous and ate at 3.30 am.

Raj Kapoor was always very precise about what he wanted. He was a musician himself and played the *tabla*, *dholak*, flute, piano, and even the violin.

NMK: It's a fabulous song and works like a story with a beginning, middle and end. A dream that turns into a nightmare, serving as a catalyst for *Awaara*'s hero. Manna Dey's singing is so evocative. You have sung so many wonderful songs with him. When did you first meet?

LM: I don't remember. But I know I met him at Anil Biswas's house.

NMK: It sounds like you met a lot of people at Anil Biswas's place!

LM: *[laughs]* Anilda was a very popular man. Charming, with a great sense of humour. He was a good singer too.

Manna Dey had a background in classical music and his uncle, K.C. Dey, was a famous singer at New Theatres in Calcutta. Sometime in the '50s, when I was singing at a concert in Nagpur with Mukesh Bhaiya, I met Pankaj Mullick who was also performing there.

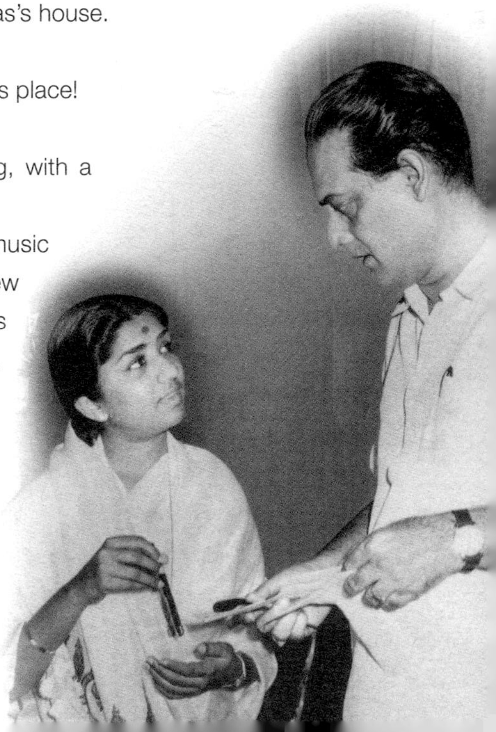

When recording a duet with singer/composer Hemant Kumar, to reach the mic, she was required to stand on a box and sing because he was much taller than her.

With Manna Dey (left) performing a symphony composed by Anthony Gonsalves (right) who was also composer Pyarelal's violin teacher. She also sang 'Ave Maria' and songs in Konkani at the show held at St. Xavier's College. 1960s.

I remember him saying: 'Sister, I want to compose songs for you.' I also met Manna Dey's uncle, K.C. Dey, at an HMV function in Calcutta and he commented: 'There's only one singer and that's Lata!'

Manna Dey is a very nice and good man. Plain-speaking. I often visited him and we frequently ate together. I talked nonsense with him and enjoyed his company. He can sing all types of compositions, but when he records songs based on classical music, these are especially good. We have sung many duets together and they have worked well. Mannada always helped me sing classical songs. Comedic songs were also his forte. His voice is deep and more mature. Unlike Rafi Sahib or Talat Sahib, who could sing for an actor of any age, Manna Dey's singing did not sound as youthful. His voice suited Raj Kapoor and Mehmood very well. What a wonderful time it was. We all worked together then, loved each other like brothers and sisters.

NMK: It must have been a glorious time. I am reminded of the wonderful duet 'Pyaar hua ikraar hua' that you sang with Manna Dey. Did you like the song's picturisation? Those haunting images of Raj Kapoor and Nargis singing under an umbrella in *Shree 420* are so moving.

LM: Yes, I liked the way the song was picturised. It's unforgettable. Raj Kapoor's three young children, Randhir, Ritu and Rishi, were featured in the song. Raj Kapoor knew what he wanted and often had Shankar-Jaikishan change entire musical interludes. This happened in 'Pyaar hua iqarar hua' too. The interlude music in the song was changed during the rehearsal.

Shankar and Jaikishan had started working in the mid-'40s with Prithviraj Kapoorji in his theatre company, Prithvi Theatres. So they were familiar with each other and had worked together for many years. Raj Sahib and Shankar-Jaikishan worked very closely. And along with lyricist Shailendraji and Hasrat Sahib, they sat for hours working on the songs. Raj Kapoor described some songs as 'poppatiya' [literally: as though sung by a parrot] — lightweight numbers that weren't very special but bound to be big hits!

NMK: Shankar-Jaikishan's background score in *Awaara* has such wonderful melodies and segments of these, I believe became the song 'O basanti pawan paagal' in *Jis Desh Mein Ganga Behti Hai*.

LM: This also happened in Salilda's *Jagte Raho*. Strains of the background music were later used by Salilda in the opening bars of his 'Aaja re pardesi' in *Madhumati*. And the song

'Ghadi ghadi mora dil dhadke' has been developed from the interlude melody in 'Aaja re pardesi.'

NMK: In *Jis Desh Mein Ganga Behti Hai*, there is the song 'Hai aag hamaare seene mein' which is sung by you, Mukesh, Geeta Dutt, Manna Dey and Mahendra Kapoor. Do you think this song can boast of having the greatest number of playback singers performing together?

LM: In the 1950s, yes. But I believe a greater number of playback singers sang together in a *qawali* for composer Shyam Sundar. There was Zohrabai, Rajkumari, Shamshad Begum, Kalyani, Hamida, her brother, Iqbal and me. These artists were well known in their time. I don't remember the title of the *qawali* or the name of the film.

In those days, I recorded songs unaware of the details of the film — when it would be released or anything like that. The only thing I asked was — which actress I was singing for, details about the character she plays in the film and at what point the song features in the story.

NMK: Another singer who had such individuality was Talat Mahmood. He started singing professionally at the age of 16, moving from Lucknow to Calcutta and finally settling in Bombay in 1949. He had such a soft and melodious voice. Did you like his singing?

LM: Yes, I did. It had a soft tone. He had excellent diction and intonation. I first met him at Anil Biswas's place where he spent much time. I can't recall the first duet I sang with Talat Sahib but there were many.

Before Talat Mahmood entered films, he sang *ghazal*s by Daag, Mir and Jigar on All India Radio. His *ghazal*s were very popular and he was well known. I particularly liked his 'Tasveer teri dil mera behla na sakegi.' It was a non-film *ghazal* by Faiyaz Hashmi. Thanks to the radio, both Talat Mahmood and Hemant Kumar became famous.

We were great fans of theirs, especially Hemant Kumar. I really liked his non-film song 'Anchal se kyun baandh liya mujh pardesi ka pyaar.' On his first visit to Bombay, I went to Hemantda's house to meet him. He asked me to sing 'Vande Mataram' for *Anandmath*. It was the first of his songs I recorded. Geeta Bali performed it on screen.

We worked together in many successful films, including Filmistan's *Nagin* — and 'Mann dole' was the first of the many songs I sang in the film. I remember singing it all through the night on a studio stage at Filmistan. It was a long and difficult night! *[smiles]*

NMK: When recording a duet with a female singer, did you help each other as you went along?

LM: When we worked on a song all the musicians and singers would rehearse together before recording it. It's not the way we work today. Now we record on multi-tracks and musicians and singers don't need to be present at the same time.

I have recorded many songs with Shamshad Begum, Zohrabai, Rajkumari Dubey, Amirbai Karnataki and Geeta Roy. The duet I sang with Amirbai Karnataki for *Samadhi*, 'Gore gore, o baanke chhore' was a big hit. It had a touch of the Rumba and the Samba. Shamshad Bai and Zohrabai were always very sweet to me and we shared a great sense of camaraderie and understanding between us.

With Nargis (left), Raj Kapoor (right), musician Chakravarty (standing) who played the khola, *discussing the music for an early Raj Kapoor film.*

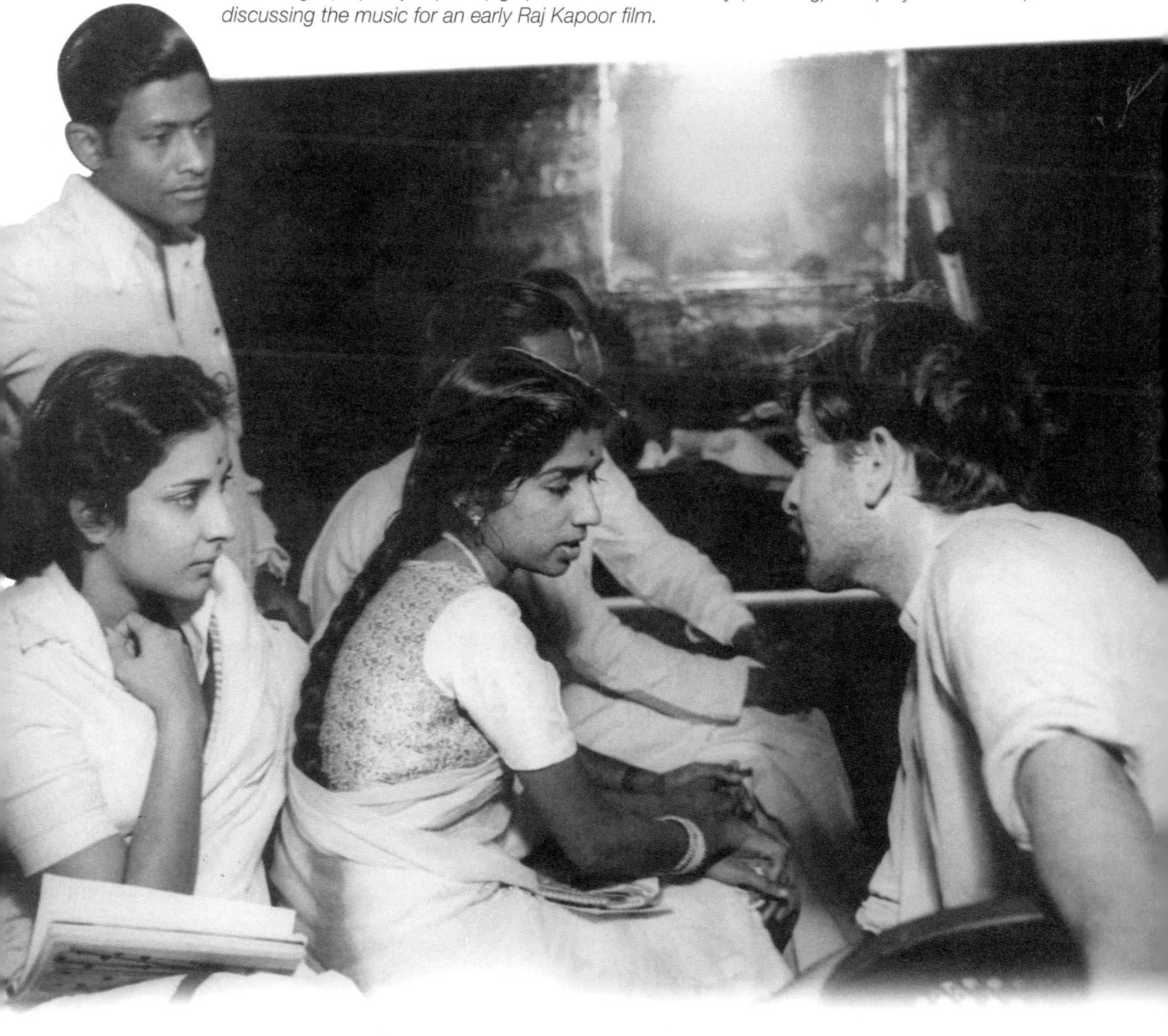

Lata Mangeshkar shared a close and at times fiery friendship with composer Jaikishan. Seen here at the Cricket Club of India, Bombay. 1960s.

NMK: Did they realise you were the top singer of the next generation and will soon be taking over? Was it as competitive as it is now?

LM: There is competitiveness in every generation. It can't be avoided. But in those days, we were close to one another. We spent time together, visited each other's homes and ate together. Some singers were probably irritated with me, and the impact my singing was having. It is human nature. It's easy to think negative thoughts of someone who you never see outside of work, with whom you never spend time or share a meal. In those days, musicians, singers and chorus singers got on well together. There was never a sense of anyone feeling superior to the other. No, never. Today there is more competitiveness because people don't have the same kind of close ties. Relationships and friendships aren't as valued as they once were.

NMK: Were there many people who were jealous of your talent?

LM: The people who loved me outnumbered those who were jealous! *[smiles]* I chose to ignore these things and get on with my work.

NMK: When the music director sings the song for you or the film director explains the filmic situation, what can you add?

LM: When I hear a song and once I know the melody, I believe it's my duty to sing it as well as possible, at least according to my own standards of good singing. I usually pay most attention to what the composer wants. I ask him: 'What if I add this *taan* or sing the words in this way?' If he thinks it's all right, then I'll sing it like that. The music director has composed the tune so it's essential to take note of what he wants.

As far as the film directors were concerned, for instance, Raj Kapoor Sahib, would tell me he wanted a *taan* in a particular song. He would say: 'I want you to sing the words like this. Linger on this note — because I will picturise the song in that way.' I have added nuances and variations in many songs. I like embellishing the song because it is a way of adding some new touch.

Composers like Madan Mohanji, Jaidevji, Shankar-Jaikishan and Laxmikant-Pyarelal encouraged me to add something of my own. Madan Mohanji used to always say: 'This is the basic mould or framework of the song. Now you sing it and adorn it. If you want to sing an *alaap* — then go ahead.'

That is how some music directors worked while others would tell me: 'Sing the song the way I have composed it.' I believe all singers must try to add something of their own.

NMK: Is your personality present in the song?

LM: Absolutely. I get completely lost in a song. But I always try to sing according to the character portrayed in the film. What kind of character is she? I think about that and also ask which actress I am singing for. When I first started singing, I didn't pay much attention to this. I paid more attention to adding nuance and variation.

Master Ghulam Haider was the first to tell me: 'Lata, pay more attention to the lyrics and who will mime the song on screen. This is important — only then will the song work better. And try to sing the words clearly so we know what they are. Be mindful of this.'

NMK: How do you go about singing in other languages?

LM: I first listen to someone who speaks the language and who reads the lyrics to me. I pay great attention to pronunciation. Once I hear the words spoken, I write the song lines phonetically in Hindi and then sing. Of course you need to ask: 'What's going on in the scene? Is the heroine crying or laughing?' With the appropriate mood in mind, I try and add feeling to the song. By the grace of God, my songs in other languages — including Bengali — have been appreciated. People say they are good and the words have been correctly pronounced.

NMK: Isn't there a famous incident in which Dilip Kumar commented on your Urdu pronunciation?

LM: I must tell you the story. One day Anil Biswas, Yusuf Bhai [Dilip Kumar] and I were travelling to work together on the train. This was in 1947 or '48. In those days, Yusuf Bhai was able to travel by train as no one reallly recognised him!

We were sitting in a compartment and Yusuf Bhai asked who I was. Anilda replied: 'She is a new singer and sings well. You'll like her voice when you hear her.' They were chatting together and Yusuf Bhai asked him: 'Where is she from?' 'She is Maharashtrian.' 'But their Urdu pronunciation isn't correct and in their singing you can smell *daal-bhaat*' [implying a Marathi accent would come through in the pronunciation of Urdu]. I felt terribly hurt hearing him say such a thing.

I knew the composer Mohammed Shafi. He was an assistant to Anil Biswas and Naushad Sahib, and a few days later, I told him I wanted to learn Urdu so I could pronounce it correctly. He found me a *maulana*, a man called Mehboob, who taught me Urdu for a short while. When I speak, my Urdu isn't very good, but when I sing I make sure there are no flaws in my diction.

Singing 'Vande Mataram' with Geeta Dutt and Anil Biswas (centre) during a performance held for an American delegation led by Frank Capra who attended India's first International Film Festival, Bombay. 1952.

NMK: I find this incident very revealing. Instead of feeling aggrieved about Dilip Kumar's comment or choosing to ignore it, you decided to take on the challenge and made sure you learned Urdu to get the pronunciation right. It shows a willingness to take criticism on board and strive towards bettering one's self — and above all, not letting a bruised ego come in the way. Learning to get it right is clearly important to you. I am sure you pay the same attention when you sing in other languages.

LM: I do try. Only people whose language it is can judge, but for my part, I try to sing the song correctly.

NMK: What counts as a good song for you?

LM: For me the most important aspect of a song is the words. The emotional content of the song is most important. The words must be well written and their meanings must match the film's narrative — this is essential. Then there's the tune. The interlude music between verses has to be good too and of course the singer must sing the song well. When all this is in place, the responsibility then falls to the film director and how well he picturises the song, and how well the actor will perform it on screen. All these elements are necessary for a song to work.

NMK: It is interesting for me to discover that with all your musical talent, you give more importance to words over tunes. Do you feel lyrics express more than dialogue?

LM: They often do. If the song is expressive, you get a clear idea of the character's inner feelings. But some songs are only used as mere padding. We are sometimes told a song will be used in this way or that, and I put all my heart into the singing. Then I see the song in the film — it's nothing. It has no impact. It just comes and goes.

At times, I have sung with a full, open-throat and when the heroine is miming on screen, she hardly opens her mouth. That looks awful!

NMK: Have you ever been pleasantly surprised by the way a song has been picturised?

LM: Yes. I have imagined many songs in a certain way and they have been filmed in a completely different way. When I see a song filmed very well, I regret not having sung it better — it might have added something more to the scene. There are also songs that I have never liked but have sung them.

NMK: Is there a difference in the way you project your voice if you're singing a song that will be filmed in an outdoor or indoor location? Does it matter?

LM: It should matter. In the late 1980s and '90s, there was a trend of adding an echo effect. We are told the heroine is singing in the intimacy of her home. But when you hear the song, it sounds as though it had ricocheted into the room from a mountaintop. *[both laugh]*

I have often argued with sound engineers and music directors and asked them: 'What are you doing? Why do you need to add so much reverb?' They say: 'It sounds good — powerful!' I tell them: 'No, it doesn't sound right. The voice should be soft.' If you are singing a lullaby, it doesn't sound appealing if it's loud and imposing.

The trend has changed, but previously high notes were sung at high pitch. I didn't like that very much. I think a lower tone is better suited particularly to sad songs.

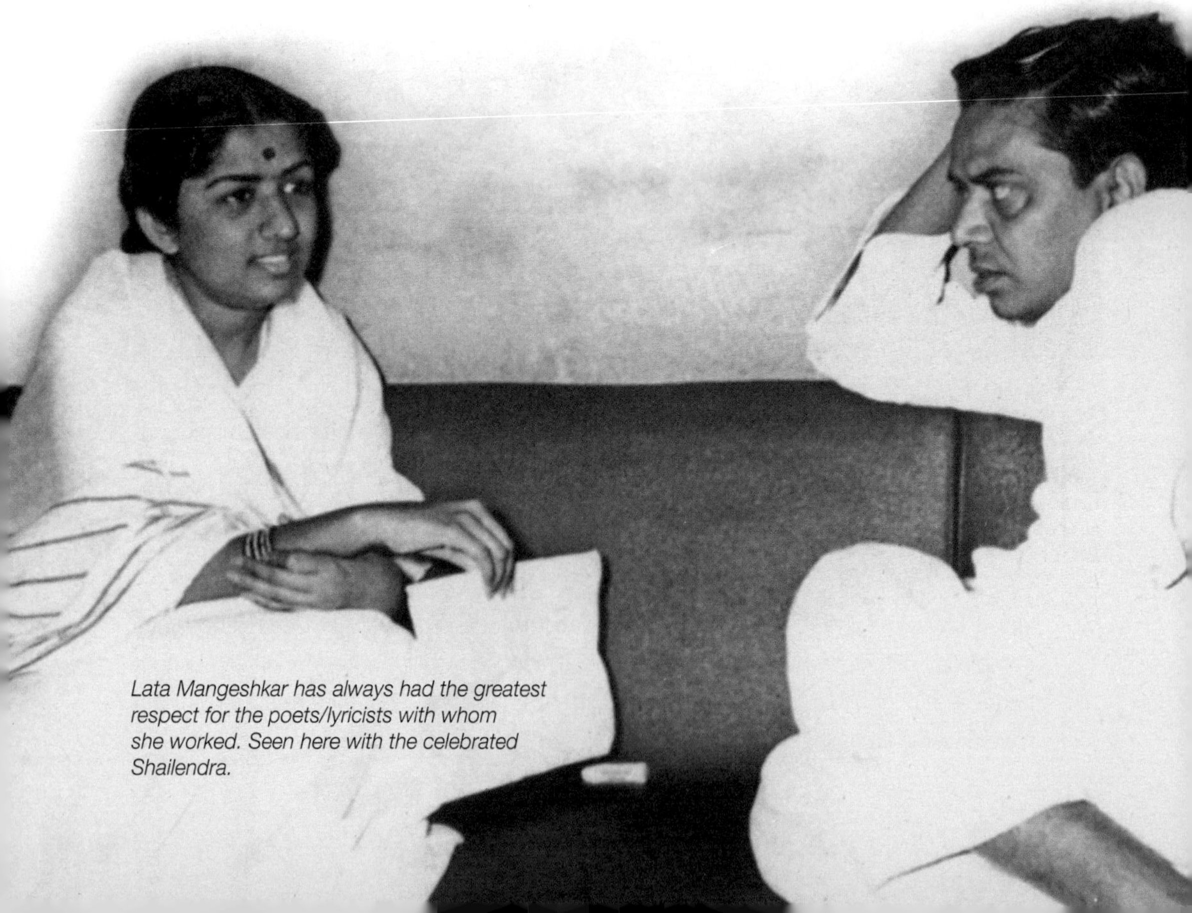

Lata Mangeshkar has always had the greatest respect for the poets/lyricists with whom she worked. Seen here with the celebrated Shailendra.

Top left: Arriving at Heathrow airport in wintry London for her first concert abroad. Top right: She was keen for her mother, Shudhhamati Mangeshkar, to see the world. Together they travelled to many countries. At a later date, they met the Queen at a garden party at Buckingham Palace. Bottom left: V.K. Krishna Menon, India's first High Commissioner to the UK came especially to London to attend a luncheon held by EMI in Lata Mangeshkar's honour. Bottom right: She receives an EMI Gold Disc. All photographs were taken in London, March 1974. Photos credit: Madan Arora.

Lata Mangeshkar was overwhelmed by the extraordinary reception she received at the Royal Albert Hall, March 1974. Dilip Kumar introduced her on the stage. Photo credit: Madan Arora.

At London's famous Royal Albert Hall in March 1974 on the morning of Lata Mangeshkar's first international concert. Photo credit: Madan Arora.

Thunderous applause greeted Lata Mangeshkar during her 1979 concert at the London Palladium. Sunil Dutt introduced her on the stage. Right: Lata Mangeshkar sang with the Wren Orchestra conducted by Ed Welch. Photos credit: Madan Arora.

Roshal Lal and his family were close friends. With Roshan's grandson, Hrithik Roshan, at a concert held to raise funds for the victims of the Gujarat earthquake. 5th May, 2001.

Top left: Lata Mangeshkar's long braided hair is a familiar sight to all her fans. Top right: At one point, she owned nine pet dogs, much to the chagrin of her mother. Above left: She accompanied Sunil Dutt during an Ajanta Arts Welfare Troupe show held for the Indian Army in Bangladesh, January, 1972. Above right: All her family have always relished her cooking.

Photograph taken by film editor Madhavrao Shinde (seen below) who taught her the techniques of still photography.

Portrait used as publicity material. Early 1960s.

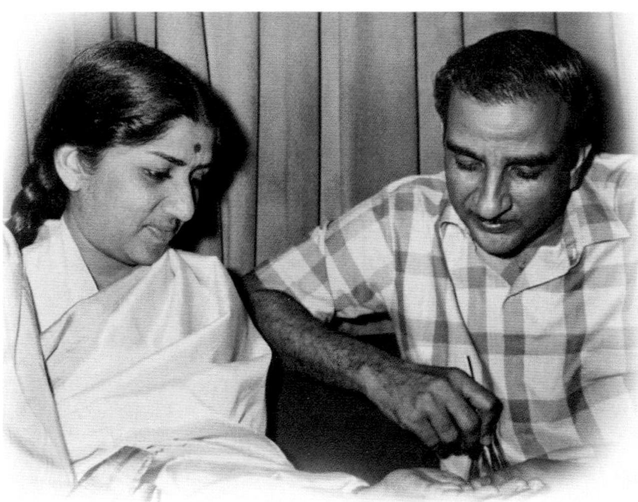

Director Raj Khosla's 1969 film Do Raaste *featured the popular song 'Bindiya chamkegi.' He also made* Woh Kaun Thi *with memorable songs by Madan Mohan.*

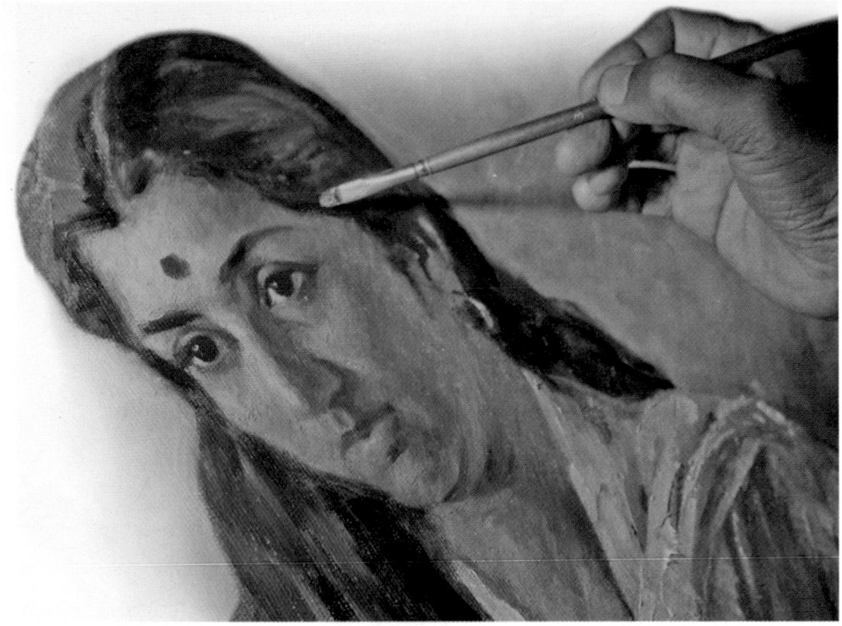

M.R. Achrekar painting a portrait of Lata Mangeshkar.

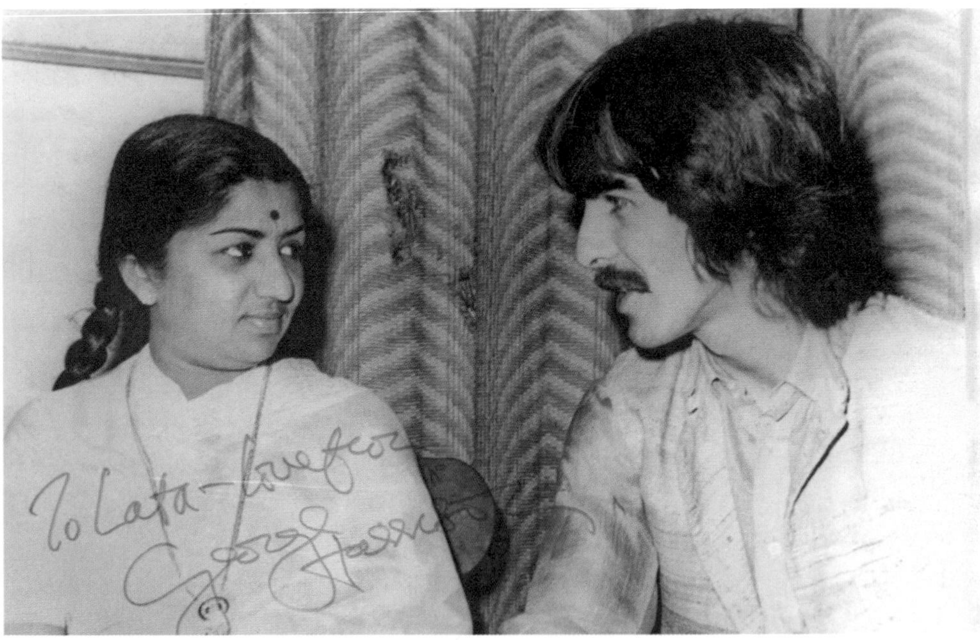

When George Harrison visited India in the 1960s, he expressly asked to meet Lata Mangeshkar. HMV Studios, Bombay.

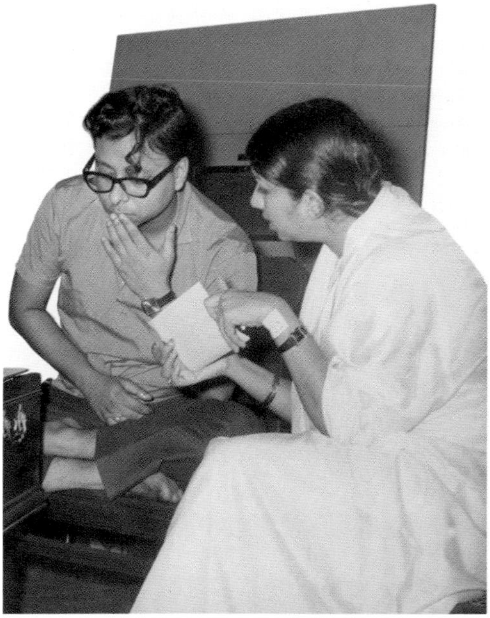

The song 'Ghar aaja ghir aaye' recorded for R.D. Burman's first film as composer (Chhote Nawab,*1961) was sung by Lata Mangeshkar.*

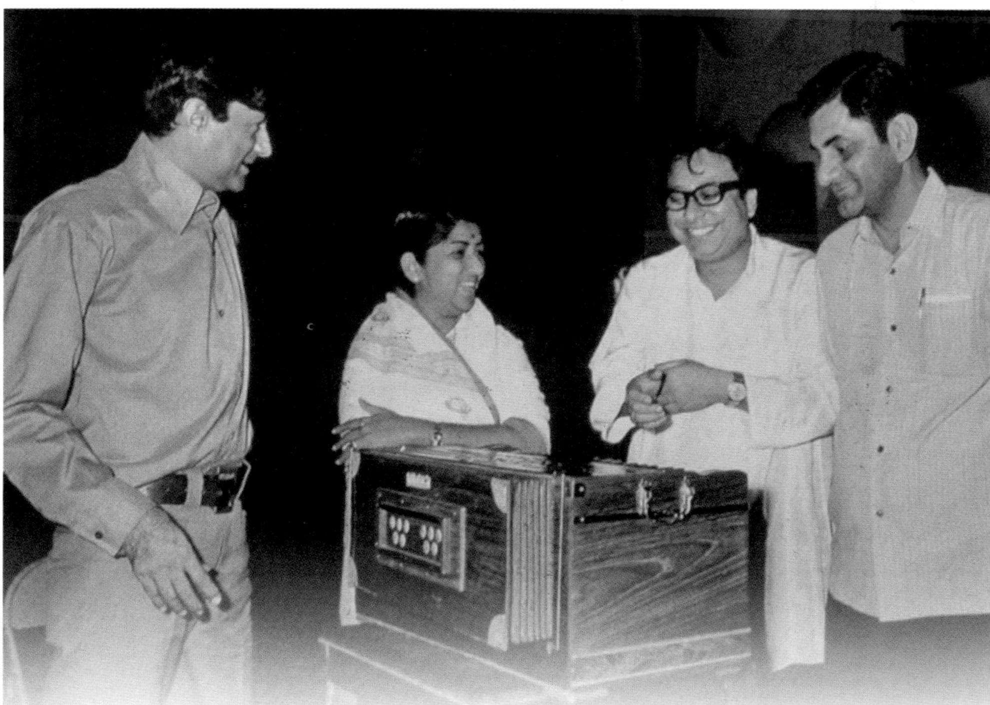

With Dev Anand (left), R.D. Burman and lyricist Anand Bakshi (far right).

Left to right: Mukesh, music director Chitragupt, Mohammed Rafi and Lata Mangeshkar rehearsing. Chitragupt was a dear friend and his sons, Anand-Milind, also work as film music composers. 1960s.

Madan Mohan's son, Sanjeev Kohli, and assistant Vikas Bhatwadekar (left) working on the songs of Veer Zaara.

NMK: For those unfamiliar with Hindi film music, can you run us through the different song types?

LM: Love songs are the most popular. The heroine is running, and the hero is running after her. *[smiles]*

We also have *ghazal*s, *qawali*s, *bhajan*s and *naat*s. Film music has a different form from the pure *ghazal* or *bhajan.* If you hear a *bhajan* composed in Raag Bahaar, it has an altogether different colour and mood. When a *bhajan* is composed for a film, it takes on a *filmi* personality.

No matter what kind of song you start off with, when it is used in a film, it will have a *filmi* effect. By that I mean the music and the words must work for the film. I have noticed this is true even for the *qawali*. The film *qawali* or *bhajan* has a different personality compared to its non-film versions. Take the *bhajan* 'Kanha kanha aan padi main tere dwaar' in *Shagird.* The heroine, Saira Banu, is sitting in front of Lord Krishna's statue as she sings. The hero is sitting nearby and even though the words of the *bhajan* are addressed to Lord Krishna, they can be understood as describing the hero's virtues. So the emphasis is on making the *bhajan* work in the story rather than it being just a devotional song.

NMK: If we take the example of 'Allah tero naam, Ishwar tero naam' [Allah is Your Name, Ishwar is Your Name] composed by Jaidev in *Hum Dono*, with excellent lyrics by Sahir Ludhianvi — would you say Jaidev was obliged to give it the colour of a film song?

LM: It's a bit *filmi*, but if you hear the whole *bhajan*, it has shades of the traditional *bhajan*. 'Allah tero naam' is unlike most film *bhajan*s. What you can identify is Jaidevji's compositional style which was often based on classical music. He knew exactly what musical instruments worked best in a song, whether *sarod* or sitar. He did not use heavy orchestration. He played the *sarod* well and gave great importance to the quality of lyrics. Jaidevji spoke Urdu and Hindi fluently and believed lyrics should say something and carry weight. Sahir Sahib excelled in this and always wrote beautiful and meaningful songs, including 'Allah tero naam.'

NMK: I am sure the great *sarod* master, Ali Akbar Khan who composed music for Navketan's *Aandhiyan* and *Humsafar*, and whom Jaidev assisted, must have influenced Jaidev. He later became S.D. Burman's assistant for many years and *Hum Dono* was his first break as composer. What made 'Allah tero naam' so right?

LM: The song flowed perfectly in the story. The young wife, played by Nanda, has exactly the right expression on her face. She is sitting with a group of women in a temple, and prays for the safe return of her husband, an army major [played by Dev Anand], who is fighting at the warfront. The other women by her side also sing for their husbands' well-being. 'Allah tero naam' is like a prayer. The wives pray for their husbands' safety but at the same time it is a message of peace. The line: 'Sab ko sanmati de Bhagwan' [Bless us all with clear minds, O Lord] is from Gandhiji's favourite *bhajan*, 'Raghupati raghav raja raam…Ishwar, Allah tero naam, sab ko sanmati de Bhagwan' [Ram, Lord of the House of the Sun. Some call You Ishwar, others call You Allah. Bless us all with clear minds, O Lord].

The *bhajan* worked well musically and dramatically in *Hum Dono*. The credit must go to Vijay Anand who made the scene so moving.

People often ask me to name my favourite film song. I suppose I have many of them. I don't even remember their titles. But I am particularly fond of devotional songs, including Meera's *bhajans* and 'Allah tero naam.'

NMK: When we hear Hindi film music over the years, we can identify an amazing variety of musical influences. What are the broad trends?

LM: Naushad Sahib introduced a lot of UP folk music. Salil Chowdhury and S.D. Burman drew on Bengali folk music. Music from Rajasthan and Maharashtra has also been used in film music. Folk music has always been very popular.

Music directors have based some songs on classical music too and this has worked well. Shankar-Jaikishan and Naushad Sahib, for example, have composed countless songs in Bhairavi — far too many in my view! I have sung so many songs in Bhairavi that I don't like the *raag* any more. But these songs were great hits, including 'Barsaat mein humse mile tum sajan' from Raj Kapoor's *Barsaat.*

The influence of Western music has been enormous since the 1980s, but the way they copy it here isn't any good. Western music is excellent but if you make a mess when copying it, you make it sound bad.

NMK: Do you enjoy Western classical music?

LM: I like listening to Mozart, Beethoven, Tchaikovsky and Chopin. I have many Western classical music albums. Salil Chowdhury had, in fact, a huge collection and he used to take me to Rhythm House in Bombay and advise me on what I should buy.

NMK: Isn't Salil Chowdhury's duet 'Itna na mujhse tu pyaar badha' from *Chhaya,* based on Mozart? Talat Mahmood also sang a solo version of the song.

LM: Yes, the song is based on Mozart's 40th Symphony in G minor.

NMK: I believe when Mozart was writing this symphony, he was facing great difficulty, growing poverty and fading popularity. Albert Einstein described the symphony's first and last movements as 'plunges into the abyss of the soul.'
Perhaps it isn't coincidence why such an emotional piece would inspire Salil Chowdhury. What for you is the basic difference between Western and Indian music?

LM: I like both traditions. I listen to Western classical music to hear how well it is composed and I listen to Indian classical to hear how well it is sung or how well it is played on say the sitar or *sarod*.

We have had, and have, exceptional classical singers and instrumentalists, including Bismillah Khan, Ali Akbar Khan, Ravi Shankar, Vilayat Khan, Allah Rakha, Zakir Hussain, Kishan Maharaj, Bade Ghulam Ali Khan, his brother Barkat Ali Khan, Bade Fateh Ali Khan, Amanat Ali Khan, the Dagar brothers, Gangubai Hangal, Pandit Bhimsen Joshi, M.S. Subbulakshmi, M. Balamurali Krishna, Rajaratnam Pillai, Ustaad Amir Khan, Salamat Ali Khan and Pandit Jasraj. My own ustaads were great singers too: Aman Ali Khan Bhendibazaarwale and Amanat Khan Devaswale. I am most probably forgetting other great artists too. We have had so many in India.

In the Indian tradition, you know we have *raag*s for different times of the day and night. Songs and music are linked to every hour and every event. Prayer is full of music too.

Indian classical music has many constraints. *Raag*s have rules and *taal*s have rules and these cannot be broken. Western classical music is a little freer. But most importantly, Western classical music has many good ideas. Mozart's ideas are very fine.

NMK: Which popular Western singers do you like?

LM: I love Nat King Cole, the Beatles, Barbra Streisand and Harry Belafonte — I was very pleased once to see Harry Belafonte perform on stage. I also like the Egyptian singer Umm Kulthum and the Lebanese singer Fairouz. Did you know the *Awaara* song 'Ghar aya mera pardesi' is based on Umm Kulthum's 'Ala balad el mahboob' [My beloved came home; it's a song from the 1936 film *Wedad*.]

A poster of Beethoven adorned her room in the Walkeshwar flat where Lata Mangeshkar lived between 1952 and 1960.

Salil Chowdhury's passion for Mozart began in his childhood. He shared his love for Western classical music with Lata Mangeshkar.

Abdel Wahab was an excellent Egyptian composer and many of his compositions were copied here. Even Naushad Sahib was 'inspired' by Abdel Wahab in the *Udan Khatola* song 'Mera salaam le jaa dil ka payaam le jaa.'

When I tour in different parts of the world, I see how popular our songs are. Our music is loved everywhere. Maybe the reason why audiences abroad react so enthusiastically to our music is because they recognise the tunes we sing and think we're singing their songs. *[both laugh]*

NMK: Every generation feels the current songs aren't as good or are less dignified than they once were. I believe this happened to you too when you sang the famous song from *Ek Thi Ladki*, composed by Vinod with lyrics by Aziz Kashmiri. By the way, was music director Vinod's real name Eric Roberts?

LM: I don't know his real name but I did know he was a Punjabi Christian. The hook line of the song 'Lara lappa lara lappa laii rakhda' is, in fact, Punjabi. The filmic situation was explained to me in great detail: this will happen and that will happen. I recorded the song and went home. Some people heard it and were angry and upset with me. 'Why did you sing this frivolous song? You shouldn't sing a song like that.' This carried on even after the film was released although it became the most popular song of *Ek Thi Ladki*. And then there was 'Gore gore, o baanke chhore.' You will be amazed to hear when I sang it at a function, many music directors came up to me and said: 'What has happened to the standard of your songs? You're singing 'Gore gore o baanke chhore' on stage?' Those songs had the reputation of being 'bad' songs. Now they are far worse. *[smiles]*

NMK: Some of your songs became the theme song for actresses. Meena Shorey, I believe, was known as 'the lara lappa' girl. And years later, Madhuri Dixit became so closely identified with 'Didi tera dewar deewana.' I suppose this was to be expected, considering the great popularity of these songs.

I am very curious about your working relationship with Rafi Sahib.

LM: Sometimes he was very chatty, and at other times he didn't say a word to me. Whenever we happened to sing a lovely duet, we laughed and joked. I teased him a lot. But he was a quiet man. How do I describe him? He was a man of God. He had no faults, no vices. He never ate *paan* or drank alcohol. He had no bad habits. He only enjoyed eating and singing. I sang so many duets with him. Some are excellent and I still like them. We have never heard as fine a voice as his, nor shall we, in the next hundred years. He had such a good voice.

I'll tell you a lovely story. It was many years ago. Mehboob Sahib's *Andaaz* had been released in 1949, in which Rafi Sahib and I sang, 'Yun to aapas mein bigadte hain khafaa hote hain.' The duet became very popular. Raj Kapoor and Nargis mimed it in the film. Rafi Sahib and I were once singing it on stage. It was a lovely song and everyone was thoroughly enjoying it. Then we came to the last lines:

Aise hans hans ke na dekhaa karo tum sab ki taraf
Log aisi hi adaaon pe fidaa hote hain

Don't smile so alluringly at passers-by
Smiles such as yours can melt many hearts

Rafi Sahib was in full flight, adding many *taans*. When he came to the last line, he sang 'Log aisi hi fidaon pe adaa hain' [Melts such as yours can smile many hearts]. The audience burst out laughing! Rafi Sahib started laughing and then I started laughing. We never managed to finish the song. We just couldn't stop laughing. They had to bring the curtain down and we went backstage. *[smiles]*

NMK: What a lovely moment! And Kishore Kumar? Was he an extraordinary personality as widely believed?

LM: Where do I start? When we were recording together, we did nothing but laugh. He never stopped. He sometimes even danced at the recording session. One day he told me a story: Dadamoni [Ashok Kumar] and his family lived in Khandwa, Madhya Pradesh. In those days, marriages were arranged, and their mother was going to see a girl for Dadamoni. Kishoreda told his mother he wanted to go with her to see his future sister-in-law. His mother was reluctant but he insisted. He poured so much oil in his hair that it was dripping down his face. *[laughs]* Off he went with his mother to the girl's place, looking hideous.

One of her favourite singers is Nat King Cole. The charcoal drawing of this great performer is by Usha Mangeshkar.

Lata Mangeshkar always believed that Mohammed Rafi was a man of God besides being an exceptional singer.

Kishoreda then told me what happened next: 'My parents were talking in the drawing room and I decided to go inside to see the girl because I thought I might be offered *rasgulla*s. When I went inside, the bride-to-be asked about me and was told — I am the boy's brother. She looked at me and shrieked: 'O Ma, he's so dark-skinned and ghastly. If this is how he is, what must his brother look like?'

He told us that they brought the girl out and Kishoreda's mother asked if she could sing. The girl's father said yes and then a harmonium was produced. And the girl began to sing. Kishoreda paused, turned to me and said: 'Lata! Do you know what she sang?' He then proceeded to imitate the poor girl and sang 'Vande Mataram' completely out of tune. *[both laugh]*

NMK: Did he make you laugh when you were actually recording?

LM: Oh yes! Sometimes I arrived late for a recording and he would be sitting there quietly. He would look at me and say: 'Lata, you're here! Come, sit down.' As soon as the music director started to rehearse the song, Kishoreda would look at me, raise his eyebrows and say under his breath: 'What do you think?' Meaning the song was no good. He just looked at me and I would burst out laughing. The music director never understood why I was laughing.

Kishoreda did all sorts of things. Many times I had to stop him and say: 'Kishoreda, please let me sing. Or else my voice will go from laughing.'

NMK: And Mukeshji. What did you like about his voice?

LM: The reason I liked his singing was because he liked K.L. Saigal. Mukesh Bhaiya had even met him and the first song he sang 'Dil jalta hai to jalne de,' composed by Anilda from *Paheli Nazar* was a carbon copy of K.L. Saigal's singing style. *[smiles]* Whenever Mukesh Bhaiya and I met, we would talk endlessly about Saigal Sahib — in fact, he was the proud owner of Saigal Sahib's harmonium which he looked after carefully.

We initially shared an admiration for this great singer but as time passed, I got to know Mukeshji better. He was a very good man. He was very fond of me and I considered him like a brother. In 1951, when he produced *Malhar,* I sang all the songs. But he lost a lot of money in the film. He later composed the music for *Anuraag,* and asked me to sing the songs, including a Kabir *doha* which was used in the title credits.

Not only did Mohammed Rafi (left), Lata Mangeshkar and Mukesh recorded thousands of songs but they also performed together in several concerts and stage shows.

Jaako rakhe saayian maar sake na koi
Baal na baanka kar sake jo jag bairi hoi

No one can ever slay a man under God's protection
Nor a hair on his head be touched even if the world opposes him

I still remember singing the *doha* and suddenly his eyes filled with tears. I asked: 'Mukesh Bhaiya, what is worrying you?' He said: 'Didi, when people are faced with problems, only true friends go out of their way to help. Seeing you here today makes me realise just how close you are to me.'

A recording session with this great singer/actor never turned out the way it was planned as Kishore Kumar kept everyone in stitches of laughter.

He accompanied me when I went on tour to America. He stood by me in every way. We were like family. In fact, I have been close to very few people in the film industry and Mukeshji was one of them.

NMK: It's interesting how your mutual love for K.L. Saigal led to such a close friendship. K.L. Saigal was of course the first star of Indian cinema. He was a talented actor and exceptional singer who died all too young in 1947 at the age of forty-two.
By the end of the 1940s, the singing-star era had virtually ended, but there was Suraiya who was still working until 1963.

LM: She was a fine artist. Suraiya hadn't been formally trained in singing but possessed a natural gift. She was a big star and it was perhaps acting that took precedence over singing. I sang a few duets with her, including 'O pardesi musafir' *[Balam]*, 'O door des se ajaa re' *[Shokhiyan]*, 'Bedard shikaari' *[Sanam]* and 'Mere chand, mere laal' *[Deewana]*.

NMK: How would you define the qualities of the female playback singers with whom you have worked?

LM: Among the older generation there was Amirbai Karnataki who passed away in 1965. She was also known as 'Kannada Kokila' and was a minor singing star before becoming a playback singer. Her elder sister, Gauharbai Karnataki, was a well-known actress. Amirabai sang many songs in the 1940s, including the famous 'Door hato ai duniyawalon, Hindustan hamaara hai,' 'Dheere dheere aa re baadal' and 'Ghar ghar mein diwali,' which were composed by Anil Biswas for *Kismet*. Zohrabai Ambalewali and Shamshad Begum were very popular too. Zohrabai's songs in *Rattan*, written by D.N. Madhok, especially 'Akhiyan milaake,' were all the rage. In fact, Naushad Sahib established himself as a leading composer of Hindi cinema following the release of *Rattan*. Zohrabai Ambalewali had a heavy full-throated voice, and to some extent you could say her singing style was similar to *ghazal* singers who usually performed in *mehfil*s.

Anil Biswas's sister, Parul Ghosh, who was married to the excellent flautist Pannalal Ghosh, also sang in many 1940s films, in which her husband composed the music.

NMK: What about Geeta Dutt?

LM: As far as her voice was concerned, she couldn't sing high notes, but didn't sing like the others. She had a very unique voice. I met Geeta for the first time when we were recording 'Jawani ki rail chali jaaye re' for *Shehnai.* She was beautiful, open and friendly. When she spoke Hindi you could hear her Bengali accent but never when she sang.

Burmanda gave Geeta many songs. He had developed a style of his own and Geeta followed his style. She always sang perfectly in tune and her diction was good too. I have always liked her song 'Waqt ne kiya kya haseen situm' in *Kaagaz ke Phool.*

NMK: What are Asha Bhosle's strengths?

LM: Asha is so versatile. She can sing all kinds of songs very well — sad songs, dance numbers and cabarets. I am not saying this because she is my sister, but it's my duty to speak about her qualities. Looking at the variety of songs she can sing, no singer can match her.

When Asha first came onto the scene, her singing was quite different — then she too came under the influence of Burmanda and developed his style further. His style was one in which stress was placed on a particular word: 'Mere ban jaao,' the word 'jaao' is stressed. He introduced this style from Bengali folk singing. O.P. Nayyar used this style as well. Remember Asha's 'Aaiye meherbaan' in *Howrah Bridge* — the way she stresses the word 'Aaiye.' That's another example. Asha sang frequently for O.P. Nayyar. He always chose Shamshad Begum, Geeta Dutt, Rafi Saab and Kishore Kumar to sing his songs. He believed his music didn't work with my voice and I agreed with him. My voice wasn't right for his compositions.

NMK: The press have talked over the years about the sibling rivalry between you and Ashaji. Is there any truth in it?

LM: Asha and I have always been close and still are. In 1947, when she was only fourteen, she wanted to marry a neighbour of ours, Ganpatrao Bhosle, who was a ration inspector. Mai was completely against the marriage. So Asha left home and married against Mai's wishes. Mai was most unhappy.

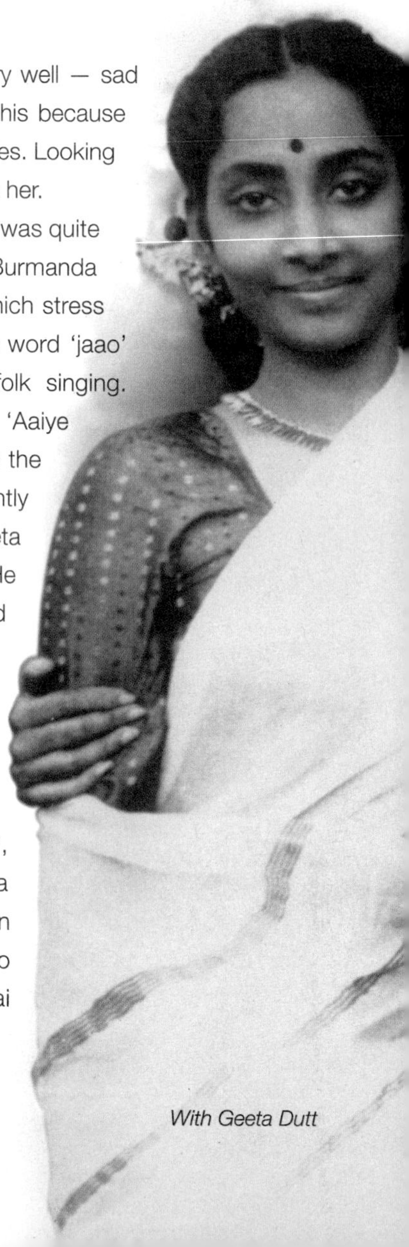

With Geeta Dutt

Once Asha was married, her husband did not want her to have anything to do with us. She wasn't allowed to see us or write to us. This was the situation for years. Ganpatrao Bhosle used to take Asha to various music directors and make her audition for them. He believed that she would earn him lots of money and wanted to control her. Asha suffered a lot during those years. She finally left her husband in 1960.

We were living in Walkeshwar at the time, and when Asha returned home, she was pregnant with her third child, Anand, whom we call 'Nandu.' We moved to Prabhu Kunj on Peddar Road soon after Asha's return, and she bought a flat on the same floor as us.

It's wrong to talk of rivalry having spoilt our relationship. We are sisters and neighbours. We talk to each other and eat together. If either of us has a problem, we tell each other. And if we have something to celebrate, we celebrate together.

NMK: Do you think you're a happy or sad person?

LM: I have always been a positive person. There wasn't much time to be anything else! I was always so busy working. To some extent, it's true people can't read my moods. I laugh and joke; I don't usually show what I am feeling inside.

NMK: Are there days when you feel low?

LM: Sometimes, yes. For no reason at all I wake up and think it's a bad day and feel depressed. Then the next day I get up and I'm happy. It's a cycle.

NMK: I wonder if it helps feeling low on a day when you happen to be recording a sad song.

LM: Maybe. But sometimes I wake up feeling happy and go to the recording studio and have to sing a mediocre and dull song. And end up feeling utterly depressed even though the day had started out well. *[both laugh]*

With sister Asha Bhonsle.

NMK: You've sung thousands of songs and worked with so many music directors. What essential techniques did you learn?

LM: I had heard many film songs and seen many movies before joining the film industry. But I believe, in earlier times, greater importance in the style of singing was given to music rather than to lyrics. And for me, the song words were always the most important.

Anil Biswas taught me many things — perhaps he didn't mean to teach me, but I remember his advice. He taught me when to inhale and exhale. So when I sing, people can't tell when I take a breath. Another thing Anilda told me was — if I am stressing a particular note — how much to fade in and out of the note. I learned these techniques from him. Perhaps other singers didn't pay much attention to this, but I did.

Ghulam Haider Sahib advised me to make sure I sing every word clearly. We must know what the words are. And if a word happens to fall on a beat — it must be emphasised a little, in order to 'lift' the song.

Through the years, I have picked up other things from various composers, but the advice of Anilda and Ghulam Haider Sahib has stayed with me.

NMK: It is indeed so easy to transcribe your songs. We know what every word is. This must also help audiences to immediately connect to a heroine's emotions because they don't need to second-guess the words you are singing. Your diction and ease in communicating the essence of the song must be greatly appreciated by lyricists and music directors.

Were there any music directors you found difficult to please?

LM: At the beginning there are difficulties with everyone. I was always apprehensive when I sang for Sajjad Hussain Sahib because he was very particular. He never liked loud singing. Sometimes an *alaap* is sung rather loudly — he didn't like that. He insisted all the musical instruments were perfectly tuned. He played the mandolin extremely well and if a single musical instrument was slightly out of tune, it displeased him. Compromising was not in his nature. I often wondered when I sang for him: 'Will he like it? Am I singing correctly?' But I always wanted to work with him. Even now when you hear his songs, though the verses are sung in a high octave, they sound effortless. They aren't painful to hear, nor do they sound as though they were strenuous for the singer. This was his approach and I found it a little difficult.

NMK: A most stunning example of what you mean about the softness at high pitch is your Sajjad Hussain song 'Ai dilrubaa nazaaren mila kuchh to mile gham ka silaa' from

Rustom Sohrab, with lyrics by Jaan Nisar Akhtar. I watched it again on YouTube. The song is so subtle and tuneful. The soundtrack of *Sangdil* by Sajjad Sahib is excellent too. And what about Naushad Sahib? You sang so often for him.

LM: Naushad Sahib was always polite and calm — you could tell he was from Lucknow. *[smiles]* Grace and elegance ran in his veins. I really liked working with him. Whenever we met, we reminisced about the past. He was a good and dignified man. He was a calm man but a perfectionist when working. Things had to be just right. He had particular habits like telling Ramlal, the *shehnai* player, to hit the note '*Ga*' *[gandhar]* with a little force when it featured in a song.

Naushad Sahib composed songs to match the ability and range of the singer. He would say: 'I know just the right notes for Lata as she can sing in high octaves. This composition is right for Rafi Sahib.' This was characteristic of Naushad Sahib. There was no problem singing his songs. But when rehearsing, he made us sing each line ten times: 'It should be like this...no, like that.'

Many of his songs were based on Indian classical music. His 'Baadal aaya jhoom ke,' sung by Shamshad Begum in *Shahjehan* is a good example of how much Arabic music has influenced Naushad Sahib.

NMK: You are absolutely right. I found this clip on YouTube and the opening bars sound just like an Umm Kulthum song — the style of singing, the use of percussion and the bank of violins playing in harmony. You mentioned Naushad Sahib's frequent use of classical music — can you easily identify which *raag* a song is based on?

LM: Yes. And if a *raag* is totally unfamiliar, I ask the composer to tell me which one he has used.

NMK: Your contribution has had an immeasurable impact on Hindi film music. By the end of the 1940s, you became *the* leading voice of Indian cinema, announcing a new era which has lasted over six decades. Your experience has been so vast. Can you recall how many composers you have worked with?

LM: When I began as a playback singer, I worked with many music directors, important ones and minor ones too. We sang for so many — I can't remember how many. Among the popular songs were Husnlal-Bhagatram's 'Chale jaana nahin' and 'Chup chup khade ho.' They were greats hits in their time. I also worked briefly with composer Shyam Sundarji who had his own style — a Punjabi, Multani style. He composed some wonderful songs in *Bazaar* like 'Saajan ki galiyan chhod chalen' and 'Bahaaren phir bhi aayengi' in *Lahore*. But I didn't sing many songs for him.

Sudhir Phadke's 'Jyoti kalash chhalake' from *Bhabhi ki Chudiyan* is another fine composition. It was written by Pandit Narendra Sharma and composed in Raag Bhopali. It's like a traditional Maharashtrian song we sing as a morning prayer to awaken the gods.

Early on in my career I sang for C. Ramchandra in *Shehnai*. C. Ramchandra recorded two versions of the song 'Aana meri jaan meri jaan Sunday ke Sunday,' one with Meena Kapoor and the other with Shamshad Begum. The song became hugely popular — despite the fact that some people thought it was frivolous.

C. Ramchandra's music in *Anarkali* was very successful. His musical style was 'sweet,' a mix of Marathi and a little Hindi. In fact, many of his songs are close to Marathi folk songs and the Maharashtrian *bhavgeet*. Latin American music was also a great influence. I believe his music was distinctive in its time.

NMK: In *Anarkali* you sing 'Zamaanaa ye samjha ke hum pi ke aye,' and in the middle of the song, singing as a drunk person, you hiccup.

LM: *[laughs]* C. Ramchandra suggested I hiccup! I don't drink but had to imagine how a drunk person might sing. I have sung quite a few 'drunk' songs, including 'Kaise rahoun chup,' which was a Laxmikant-Pyarelal song in *Inteqaam*.

NMK: I believe Abdul Halim Jaffar Khan played the sitar in C. Ramchandra's 'Ye zindagi usi ki hai jo kisi ka ho gaya,' in *Anarkali*. Is this right?

LM: Yes, he did. Ustaad Ali Akbar Khan played the *sarod* in the *Seema* song 'Suno chhoti si gudiya ki lambi kahaani' and Pannalal Ghosh played the flute in the *Basant Bahaar* song 'Main piya teri tu maane ya na maane' — composed by Shankar-Jaikishan.

From the 1950s, there were several classical musicians who played in film music, including Ustaad Ali Akbar Khan, Ustaad Abdul Halim Jaffar Khan, Pannalal Ghosh, Ramnarayan and Ustaad Allah Rakha. Ustaad Allah Rakha even composed music for a few films in the 1950s under his real name, A.R. Qureshi.

Vilayat Khan's nephew, Rais Khan, who is a good singer too, played the sitar in many of my songs. My favourite instrument is, in fact, the sitar.

NMK: Did you ever work with Bismillah Khan?

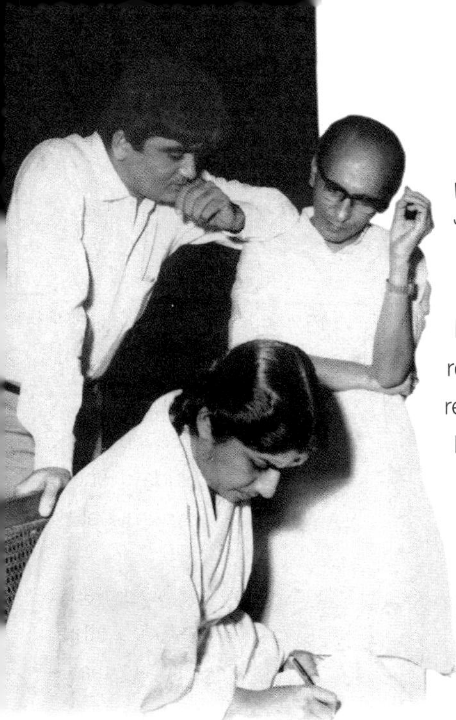

With Sunil Dutt (left) and Jaidev during the song recording for Mujhe Jeene Do *(1963).*

LM: We never actually worked together as he had already recorded the *shehnai* tracks in *Goonj Uthi Shehnai* and I recorded the songs later. He composed the tune for 'Dil ka khilona haaye toot gaya.' He was a very lively and interesting man and a fine musician.

I met Bade Ghulam Ali Khan too. He was such a good man. If he saw light shine in a particular way, he would say: 'I will sing Malkauns.' I also met M.S. Subbulakshmi who was a very fine lady. I met many classical singers, including Kesarbai Kerkar, Girija Devi, Siddheswari Devi and Begum Akhtar. Begum Akhtar was particularly nice to me.

NMK: I believe Bade Ghulam Ali Khan made a very interesting comment about you.

LM: Yes. I once read an interview of Pandit Jasraj's — in which he said he was with Bade Ghulam Ali Khan Sahib in the 1950s and one day from some distance, my song 'Ye zindagi usi ki hai jo kisi ka ho gaya' could be heard. Khan Sahib told everyone to be quiet so he could listen to it. Then he said with affection: 'Kambakht, kabhi besuri nahin hoti' [The blessed girl never sings out of tune]. *[both laugh]*

NMK: Pandit Ravi Shankar's work for Satyajit Ray is well known but he also wrote music for Hindi films, including K.A. Abbas's *Dharti ke Lal,* Chetan Anand's *Neecha Nagar*, Hrishikesh Mukherjee's *Anuradha*, Trilok Jetley's *Godaan*, and Gulzar's *Meera*. Was there anything different about singing under the direction of a classical musician like Pandit Ravi Shankar?

LM: He worked very hard and during the rehearsals, he was quite particular about the singing style. I sang most of the songs in *Anuradha*, and they were very popular. I sang one song in *Godaan* as well. The *Anuradha* songs were based on light classical music. I don't recall if we needed many retakes.

Recording for Pandit Ravi Shankar was not like recording for Naushad Sahib. Whenever we finished recording a duet for him, at the end of the take, my co-singer and

I would look at each other and, pre-empting Naushad Sahib, we would say in unison: 'Excellent! One more!' *[both laugh]*

NMK: What about the key Bengali music composers who worked in Hindi cinema? How would you describe their music?

LM: I don't remember for certain, but I think S.D. Burman started working in films before I did. I remember Salil Chowdhury joining films during my time, as did Hemant Kumar.

Salilda's way of composing songs was unique and influenced by Bengali folk music. He sang and had a musical group. In fact, Hemant Kumar recorded some of Salilda's non-film Bengali songs and they were big hits in Calcutta, including 'Palki chale' and 'Ranar' [Runner].

'Ranar' is based on a poem by Sukanta Bhattacharya, one of the most honoured Bengali poets. He was a communist and died when he was twenty. The poem is about a poor postman who carries letters and money orders from one post office to another. He works at night and his job is exhausting. The poem was set to music by Salilda, and Hemant Kumar sang it. The song was much loved.

With the renowned singer Bade Ghulam Ali Khan.

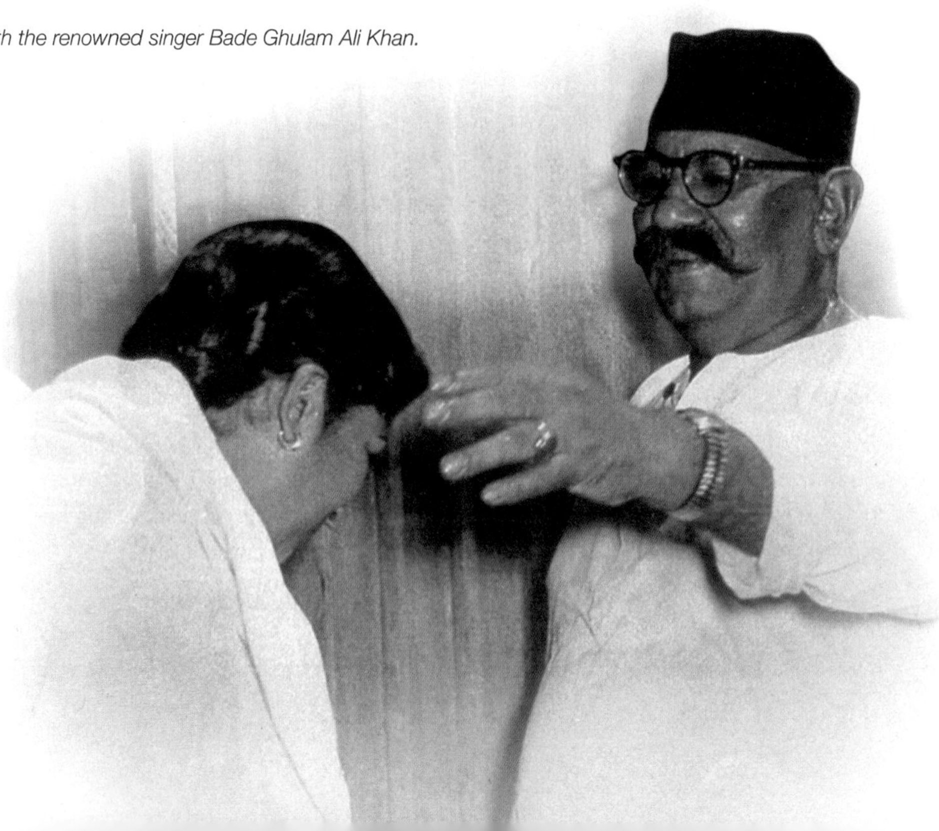

I couldn't at first guess the kind of film music Salilda would compose. I thought it would be mostly folk music, but if you listen to his compositions in *Madhumati* — they are so unusual.

NMK: I always felt there is a certain similarity between *Mahal* and *Madhumati*. Though their stories develop quite differently, both films start in similar settings. A terrible storm is raging and the hero in *Mahal* and *Madhumati* take shelter in an old dilapidated house and discover a painting that stirs up a distant past, another lifetime. 'Aayega aanewala' and 'Aaja re pardesi' are also used in both films to create the same effect — evoking a romantic past and spiritual bond between hero and heroine. Was 'Aaja re pardesi' a difficult song to get right?

LM: Actually it was recorded very quickly. I don't think it took more than a few hours. Shailendraji was very happy with the way I sang it, so he gave me a huge bunch of flowers! And Bimalda [Bimal Roy] held my hand in appreciation.

I was fond of Salilda's compositions because they were very difficult. Whether based on folk music or his imagination, his songs had so many high and low notes that sometimes the musicians would get flustered. But I enjoyed singing for him.

NMK: Hemant Kumar was such a fine singer. Do you think that influenced his compositions?

LM: Music takes on a different colour when a good singer composes it. Hemantda and I had a very good relationship. I often visited him and he would tell me: 'Look Lata, this is what I want.' It was never difficult singing his songs. He believed in a simple tune and good lyrics like 'Kahin deep jale kahin dil' or 'O beqaraar dil.' He did not believe in much orchestration. His music was straightforward. His compositions were simple and unfussy.

NMK: I read you were very unwell at the time you were recording the *Bees Saal Baad* song 'Kahin deep jale kahin dil.'

LM: In 1962, I fell very ill for about three months. I thought I would never be able to sing again. One day, I woke up feeling very uneasy in my stomach. And then I started throwing up — it was terrible, the vomit was a greenish colour. The doctor came and even brought an x-ray machine home because I could not move. He x-rayed my stomach and said I was being slowly poisoned. We had a servant in the house who made the food. Usha went straight into the kitchen and told everyone that from that moment on, she would do the cooking instead. The servant sneaked off without telling anyone and without collecting any pay. So we thought someone had planted him there. We didn't know who it was. I was bed-ridden for three months and was so weak.

I will never forget Majrooh Sahib's kindness to me during those difficult times. He came at six in the evening and sat by me every day for three long months. He ate whatever I ate and recited poetry and read me stories. We talked and laughed together. I thoroughly enjoyed his company.

When I was feeling well enough to sing, the first song I recorded was Hemant Kumar's 'Kahin deep jale kahin dil.'

NMK: Did you ever find out who was behind this?

LM: No.

NMK: Talking about good singers like Hemant Kumar who turn to composing, what about the 1960s films in which you wrote the music? How did that come about?

LM: The Marathi filmmaker Bhalji Pendharkar was a close family friend and one day he called me and said he was making *Mohityanchi Manjula*, a historical drama based on Shivaji Maharaj. He had asked a few music directors to work on the film but they were busy. Bhalji Baba was in a hurry to start production and I suggested he let me write the music. He was reluctant because he believed if the film didn't do well, the press might end up criticising me. I had a big name in playback singing and he didn't want that to happen. I told him I could compose under a pseudonym. He suggested the name 'Jatashankar.' But I didn't like it very much.

In the writings of Marathi poet-saint Shri Ramdas Swami, he makes reference to 'Anandghan,' which means 'Clouds of Happiness.' So I suggested the pseudonym 'Anandghan' and Bhalji Baba agreed. While we were discussing the film on the telephone, he recited a few lines of the song 'Neelya aabhali.' I immediately thought of a tune and sang the words back to him.

When I started working on *Mohityanchi Manjula*, I wanted Hridaynath to conduct the music and assist me, but he was away in Hyderabad. So I asked the Marathi composer, Datta Davjekar, to work with me on condition no one must know I was composing music for a film.

Davjekarji and I went back a long time to the days when I was fifteen and we were both working for Master Vinayak. He wrote the music for the Marathi films in which I had acted. In fact, Davjekarji composed the first Hindi song I ever sang in playback: 'Paa laagoo kar jori re, shyam mause na khelo hori.' The song was a *thumri* in Raag Piloo and featured in Vasant Joglekar's *Aap ki Seva Mein*.

Prior to that, in 1942, I had, in fact, recorded 'Naachu ya gade khelu saari mani haus bhari,' a song for another Joglekar film in Marathi called *Kiti Hasaal*. But it was dropped from the film. My voice was thin. I was just too young when it was recorded. Moreover, my father was not too happy about my singing for films.

NMK: How did you enjoy composing? What was it like directing singers for the first time?

LM: Hridaynath, Usha, and Asha sang in *Mohityanchi Manjula*, so there was no problem. I sang some songs too. I pay entire attention to everything I do. I composed music to the lyrics and as the story of *Mohityanchi Manjula* was a historical drama, I tried using traditional musical instruments like the *sarod*, sitar and flute.

I wrote the music for four Bhalji Pendharkar films that were made in Marathi. Jagdish Khebulkar, the poetess Shanta Shelke, and Bhalji Baba, who used the pseudonym 'Yogesh,' wrote the lyrics.

After *Mohityanchi Manjula*, I worked on *Maratha Tikuka Melvava, Sadhi Manse* and *Tambdi Maati*. The first two were historical dramas, and the others were village stories.

No one knew I was composing film music. But then *Sadhi Manse* went on to win eight Maharashtrian state awards, including Best Director, Best Singer, Best Story and Best Music.

On the night of the awards ceremony when the award for Best Singer was announced for 'Airanichya deva tula,' I went onto the stage and accepted my award. And then the Best Music award was announced, I stayed firmly in my seat. The master of ceremonies explained the music composer 'Anandghan' was none other than Lata Mangeshkar. So I was forced to publicly accept the award.

After *Tambdi Maati*, I stopped composing. At one point, I thought Hridaynath and I could become a composing duo like Shankar-Jaikishan, but my brother was not very keen. So, we dropped the idea.

Some years later, Hrishikesh Mukherjee asked me to compose music for his film *Anand*, but I politely refused. I was not keen on composing any more. I did not really have the time and was so busy recording. I told Hrishida some time later I was glad I had refused *Anand* because Salil Chowdhury wrote beautiful music for the film.

NMK: Did you compose the soundtrack of the 1950 Marathi film *Ram Ram Pavhana* under your own name?

LM: After Master Vinayak passed away, one of his assistants at Prafulla Pictures, Dinkar Patil, who later became a well-known director, and film editor, Madhavrao Shinde, found themselves out of work. So we three decided to make our first film. I was living in Bombay and they asked me to write the score. Meena also sang in the film. When *Ram Ram Pavhana* was released, it became a super hit but the music was not greatly appreciated. *[laughs]* It put me off composing. We started working on the film score in 1948/49 and at that point, I frankly did not have enough experience in film music.

NMK: I believe you also produced films?

LM: Yes, I have but I didn't enjoy it at all!

NMK: I was wondering if you could tell me something about S.D. Burman?

LM: He was a composer like no other. But he was always anxious. I sometimes suffered from sinus problems and could not record. And this would make Burmanda panic: 'What will happen to my song if Lata doesn't show up?' Worrying was in his nature.

When he taught us a song, he sang in a Bengali folk-style. His voice broke a little and was quite unique — and we found it difficult to sing like him — I mean I couldn't. I used to ask him: 'How do I sing this?' And he explained: 'Try it this way, it will sound good.'

When he was happy, he would pat me on the back and say: 'Stay happy, Lata.' When he was very pleased, he would offer me a *paan*. *[smiles]* He was a great *paan* eater and had a *paan* box with him at all times, but never offered any. And if he offered someone a *paan*, you understood he was pleased with that person.

NMK: There was a rumour you had a rift with S.D. Burman which lasted five years. Is it true?

LM: I sang a song for a Nargisji film called *Miss India*. S.D. Burman asked me to sing it softly to create a sweet mood. A few days later, he called and said we had to re-record it. I asked: 'Dada, what's wrong with it?' He explained the character who would sing in the film was a kind of tomboy and the song was too soft and feminine. So I said: 'Fine. I'll do it again but I am a little busy right now.' Two or three days later, he sent someone to arrange a recording date. I later discovered this person went to Dada, and instead of saying I was busy, he said I had refused to re-record the song. Dada was upset and assumed I was being difficult and commented that he would not work with me again. I called him and said: 'I'll spare you the embarrassment, Dada. You don't need to say anything. I won't sing for you.'

It was a misunderstanding rather than a rift. As far as I recall, R.D. Burman and Bimal Roy encouraged us to work together again. The first song we then recorded was 'Mora gora ang lai le' for *Bandini.*

NMK: Did S.D. Burman speak good Hindi and Urdu? I once interviewed Kaifi Azmi, who laughed when he remembered S.D. Burman would say 'haalfil,' instead of 'filhaal' [for the moment]!

LM: *[laughs]* S.D. Burman's Hindi or Urdu wasn't very good. However, he did understand the meaning of the song words even though he didn't speak the language perfectly. But we singers understood what he was saying. He talked to us in English as well.

NMK: You had a long association with Shankar-Jaikishan and sang such marvellous songs for them, especially in Raj Kapoor's films.

LM: There's so much to say about them. Actually, it was Anil Biswas who introduced me to Raj Kapoor. Before RK Films moved to Chembur, they used to rent offices above Famous in Mahalakshmi.

One day I was recording 'Kab aaoge balama, baras baras badali bhi bekaar gayi' for *Gajre*, and Anilda decided to call Raj Sahib down to the recording studio to hear me sing.

I was living in Nanachowk and a few days after I had met Raj Kapoor, a fair, slim, handsome young man came to see me. He said: 'You have been asked to sing some songs for Raj Kapoor.' I had seen Prithviraj Kapoorji in Kolhapur and thought he was very handsome. So I wondered how his children would be. I told my sister Meena: 'Raj Kapoor sent someone over. Perhaps it was his office boy. He was so handsome — maybe the people who work for RK are as good-looking as the Kapoors.'

When I went to the RK office in Mahalakshmi, I discovered the good-looking 'office boy' was Jaikishan! *[laughs]* I sat down a little embarassed and was formally introduced to them: 'This is Jaikishanji and Shankarji.'

The first of their songs I sang was 'Jiya beqaraar hai.' We recorded it at Famous in Tardeo — it took the whole day. In fact, all the *Barsaat* songs were recorded there.

After that we became very close friends. Jaikishan, Shankar, Hasrat Jaipuri, Shailendraji and I spent a lot of time together. Our rehearsals started at 8 in the morning and the whole day would pass in recording and arguing — we fought a lot too. Once the quarrelling was done, we ate ice cream! We used to go to Chowpatty and eat *bhel*. We never harboured any bad feelings towards each other, but I often argued with Jaikishan over small things. We once argued about the *Filmfare* awards.

NMK: I believe the *Filmfare* awards were first introduced in 1954 and initially the Best Music award was given to a particular song, not to the whole album. In 1954, Naushad Ali won the award for 'Tu ganga ki mauj main' sung by Mohammed Rafi in *Baiju Bawra.* In 1955, S.D. Burman won it for 'Jayen to jayen kahan.' It was sung by Talat Mahmood in *Taxi Driver*. From 1956, the Best Music award was given to the music director for the whole album. That year's winner was Hemant Kumar for *Nagin*.

Then Shankar-Jaikishan won the award in 1957. Was your argument with Jaikishan somewhat connected to that event?

LM: Shankar-Jaikishan were told by *Filmfare* that they would get the [1957] award for Best Music for *Chori Chori*. Jaikishan came to see me and said: 'We're getting the award so you must sing 'Rasik balma' at the awards ceremony. I said: 'I won't sing.' 'Why won't you? We're getting an award.' '*You* are getting the award, not me. The award is for Best Music. They aren't giving the award to the singer or lyricist. So why don't you let your orchestra play the tune without words and singer?' We had a big fight and he said: 'How can you talk to me like this? I'm going.' I said: 'Very well. Go!'

Then Shankarji came and said: 'Lataji, he's naïve and young. Don't be upset by what he says.' I explained to Shankarji why I had refused. 'I won't sing unless *Filmfare*

S.D. Burman always offered her a paan if he was happy with the way she recorded one of his songs.

introduces awards for playback singers and songwriters. Then I'll come. Otherwise I won't.' These were the kinds of quarrels we had.

NMK: I wonder whether people misunderstood your intentions – when it clearly led to future recognition of all singers and lyricists.

Filmfare finally introduced additional awards for Best Singer and Best Lyricist in 1959. The first recipient was Shailendra for the lovely *Yahudi* song 'Ye mera diwaanapan hai' sung by Mukesh, and you won the Best Playback Singer award for 'Aaja re pardesi' (*Madhumati*,1958). Surprisingly it was only in 1967 that *Filmfare* introduced separate awards for female and male playback singer.

How did your personal relationships impact on your professional ones? Do you believe friendship can encourage and foster better creative understanding?

LM: Why not? I was very close to many composers. Everyone has flaws but we were accepting of each other. As I mentioned to you, Madan Mohanji was like a brother to me. Salilda was very fond of me and come to think of it, I had good relations with most music directors and singers. Many of them regarded me like a sister. For instance, whenever I was recording at Mehboob Studio for Chitragupt who lived very close to the studio in Bandra, I would go to his house for lunch.

NMK: The most famous argument written about extensively was the one you had with Rafi Sahib. How did this happen?

LM: The argument with Rafi Sahib was over royalties, and took place sometime in the '60s. I felt we singers should be paid a royalty by the record companies. The other singers, including Mukeshji, Talat Mahmood, Kishore Kumar, Manna Dey fought alongside me.

Rafi Sahib and Asha believed that once a song was recorded and the producer had paid us – that was the end of it. Rafi Sahib didn't think that we should fight for royalties. This created a rift between us. From 1963 to 1967, we did not sing together. Rafi Sahib sent me a letter some time later and said he had spoken in haste. Finally it was S.D. Burman who brought us together. An S.D. Burman night was held at Shanmukhananda Hall in 1967 and Rafi Sahib and I met on the stage. We were both very pleased to be singing together again and sang the *Jewel Thief* duet 'Dil pukaare.' Nargisji and various music directors introduced Dada's songs. It was even announced that Rafi Sahib and I had made up. The audience greeted the news with much excitement!

NMK: It's indeed a shame the question of royalties was the cause of the quarrel because it sounds like forward-thinking on your part and once again, your actions benefited all singers in the long run. In most countries, musicians and singers depend entirely on royalties and these are rightfully due to them. When musicians and performers are no more, their families also depend on royalties. But I am sure it was comforting to know things had been resolved with Rafi Sahib and you were singing again with this most wonderful singer.

What about Shankar-Jaikishan, did your arguments create long-term problems?

LM: No, we may have argued many times but were very close. Our quarrels didn't last long. We sisters would sometimes play jokes on them. We invited them on Holi and when they arrived in their best suits, we sprayed colour all over them. We were all so young.

I believe no one can equal the music composed by Shankar-Jaikishan. They composed classical songs, cabarets, dance numbers, love songs, sad and happy songs. Few composers have been able to match their range. Their music has extended the life of many films — films that would have otherwise been forgotten. So many of their films enjoyed a twenty-five week run. I would tease them and say their initials, 'SJ,' did not stand for Shankar-Jaikishan, but for 'Silver Jubilee.' *[smiles]*

NMK: For those unfamiliar with the process of how you learn a song, can you explain what is involved?

LM: I first write the lyrics in Hindi, in Devnagari — even if the words are in Urdu or any other language. The music director sings the song to me so I hear the tune as I read the words. I make notes on my page of lyrics, indicating at what point I might stress a particular word. Then I memorise the tune and sing it.

Lata Mangeshkar first saw Prithviraj Kapoor in Kolhapur when she was very young. She was struck by his impressive personality.

NMK: Unlike in the West, Indian musicians don't seem to use a music sheet. Is music ever notated for Hindi film music?

LM: None of us singers work from a music sheet. Once the music director sings the tune to me, I learn it and memorise it. If you memorise a song, you internalise it — and it becomes one with your feelings. You make the song your own when you commit it to memory. When I know the tune, I am ready to record. And during the take, I add expression and feeling to the singing. If you see me performing on stage, you will see all I have in front of me are pages of lyrics — the tune is completely familiar to me. This is the general practice for all playback singers.

NMK: What about the musicians?

LM: Indian musicians don't use music sheets. Neither do classical musicians. Musicians who play Western instruments such as the violin, cello or saxophone may use music sheets when recording. Some musicians read Western notation and others Indian notation. I can't read Western notation but I know Indian notation.

NMK: Can you explain to me the purpose of a dummy track?

LM: Say if I am unavailable on a particular day, the musicians will go ahead and record the song and a singer will sing it on a separate track which is called the 'dummy track.' When I ultimately record the song, my voice will replace the demo singer.

Many years ago, Kavitha Krishnamurthy had recorded a dummy track for me. When I heard it, I thought she sang the song so well and said they should keep her version, which they did. I heard this helped her get a break in playback singing in the early days of her career.

NMK: You once talked about the difficulty of singing the song 'Ehsaan tera hoga mujh par,' from the movie *Junglee*. Why was that?

LM: Yes. At first Rafi Sahib's version was meant to be the only one in the film. Then it was decided that Saira Banu would also sing the same song. I remember seeing the cut film and found it very amusing to see Saira Banu lip-synching to Rafi Sahib's voice! So when it came to recording the song, I used Rafi Sahib's version as the dummy track.

It was a difficult song because it had many high notes. The range of a male voice is much higher — and no one could sing as well in higher octaves as Rafi Sahib — so it was difficult to sing.

NMK: I believe a violinist plays alongside you when you sing. Why?

LM: When I sing, a violinist known as a 'song violinist' sits near me and plays the entire melody while I go for a take. This is to ensure that the singer sings tunefully and in the right key. You can hear the violin in some song recordings.

In the early days, Naushad Saab had a *sarangi,* violin and organ playing alongside the singers.

NMK: Isn't the role of the *tanpura* in classical music based on the same principle? To ensure the singer sings in key?

LM: Yes.

NMK: How many times do you hear the composer sing the song before you can memorise the tune well enough to record it?

LM: I usually hear the tune once and sometimes I hear it twice.

NMK: Extraordinary! Now I understand why so many music directors speak of your great talent for instantly 'grasping' the tune. I've been at recording sessions in which the singers have needed to hear the tune quite a few times before they are actually ready to record the song.

I believe you always write 'Shri' at the top of every song page. And you never wear shoes when recording.

LM: I start all my letters with 'Shri.' Most Maharashtrians do the same — only letters of condolence won't have a 'Shri' written at the top of the page.

It's true when I sing I never wear shoes. My father believed singing was like entering a temple of Goddess Saraswati. Singing is like prayer to me. If you enter a temple, you remove your shoes as a sign of respect. So when recording or singing on stage, I always take my shoes off.

I remember when we were at the Royal Albert Hall in London for three charity concerts organised on 11, 12 and 14 March, 1974 by the India League in aid of the

Nehru Memorial Fund — Hridaynath was the concert director. The Albert Hall is one of those old, large and chilly places, and as I was about to go onto the stage, Dilip Kumar who was there to introduce me, saw me removing my sandals. He was flabbergasted and said: 'Arre tum chappal utaar rehi ho? [You're taking your sandals off!] You will die of cold!' I laughed, removed my sandals, and wearing my socks I went onto the stage of the Royal Albert Hall and sang for hours.

NMK: The London-based S.N. Gourisaria, described to me your extraordinary success. How every seat [plus 600 standing] was occupied at the Royal Albert Hall which has a capacity of 6000. Indians and Pakistanis came from all over Britain to see you.

Now there are many shows to entertain the NRIs in the UK, but there were virtually none in the 1970s. Your presence must have overjoyed them.

LM: I was very happy doing the concert but was also very nervous. It was my first show abroad. Prior to that time, I heard shows were held in cinema halls in the UK. And to imagine this was my first concert abroad and at the Royal Albert Hall no less.

NMK: You gave your first public performance alongside your father when you were nine. He would have been so proud to see you on the Royal Albert Hall stage. Did you miss him at that moment?

LM: Yes, I thought of him. But honestly he is never far from my mind.

NMK: I have listened to the wonderful double album, 'Lata Mangeshkar. Live at the Royal Albert Hall, London,' produced by V.K. Dubey of HMV and released in 1974. Dilip Kumar introduced you as his 'little sister who has a voice that defies description and definition.' You also performed later at Madison Square Garden. Did you find a difference between audiences in the UK and the US?

LM: Things have changed now but I think audiences in the UK were warmer.

NMK: In 1974, you were presented with a Gold Disc by EMI, London for being the most recorded artiste in the world. You were the first Indian artist to receive the Gold Disc. I believe the celebrated political figure and India's first High Commissioner to the UK, V.K. Krishna Menon, came to London to attend the EMI press luncheon held on 8th March, 1974, at Selfridges Hotel in your honour. Did you get much time to talk to him?

LM: He was a prominent member of the India League who organised the concert, along with Lalit Sen. He didn't talk very much to me but sent me a message saying I should wear socks! It was March and cold in England. I think he also sent me a Burberry coat to wear during my stay.

NMK: You returned again to London in 1979 to perform at the London Palladium. This time you were accompanied by Sunil Dutt and Nargis. There's a lovely picture of you standing in front of the theatre where *The King and I* was playing. Did you see *The King and I* on the London stage?

LM: No, I saw it in New York on Broadway in 1977. It had Yul Brynner and Mary Beth Peil. Seeing Yul Brynner live was wonderful. I love stage musicals.

I even saw the great Marlene Dietrich singing on stage. I will never forget her in the excellent *Witness for the Prosecution*. I also saw Ingrid Bergman in the play, *The Constant Wife*. I have always loved her.

NMK: She was wonderful. In fact, both Nargis and Nutan had a touch of Ingrid Bergman.

LM: Nargisji liked her a lot too, and to some extent, she was influenced by Ingrid Bergman. You can see that influence in some of her films.

NMK: Coming back to your travels abroad, in 1979 you performed again at the Royal Albert Hall, this time with the Wren Orchestra led by Ed Welch. How was that experience for you?

LM: It was wonderful. I sang many songs, including Meera's *bhajans*. Ed Welch rang me in London before the concert and wanted me to explain the word meanings of the *bhajan* 'Chala Vaahi Des.' I explained how the song describes Meerabai leaving behind the material world and becoming one with God. Ed Welch composed a beautiful piece for the ending of the *bhajan*.

NMK: Did the Wren Orchestra have music sheets?

LM: Yes. I sent Anil Mohile and Amar Haldipur to London and they spent days writing out all the songs in Western notation. The British musicians played very well. And the concert was a very big success.

NMK: Coming back to your work with different music directors, when speaking of them, you always mention Vasant Desai.

LM: I think he was a very good music director. He was influenced by Marathi music. In the 1940s, he worked at Prabhat Film Company in Poona and when V. Shantaramji moved to Bombay, Vasant Desai accompanied him. I considered him to be my *rakhi* brother and knew him for many years. We got on well. He composed music for a few Marathi films in which I had acted. He also worked for a time as assistant to the great *khayal* vocalist, Master Krishnarao, who was an actor and composer in Marathi cinema. Vasant Desai organised many musical programmes with all the great singers of India. He worked with the best *tabla* and *sarangi* players and got on well with all the musicians. He preferred working with singers who had a grounding in classical music because the quality of singing is better.

NMK: The other music director who had such a lovely style was Roshan.

LM: He had what you can call a 'madhur,' honey-like sound. His songs are excellent. I particularly liked the music of *Taj Mahal* and *Chitralekha.* I love his 'Paon chhu lene do.' *Mamta* had some lovely songs too, including 'Chhupa lo yun dil mein,' 'Rahte the kabhi jinke dil mein' and 'Rahen na rahen hum meheka karenge.' Like all talented music directors, he looked to Indian classical music as his source and preferred using Indian musical instruments. He played the *dilruba* and the way he used the flute in his compositions was so effective.

I like the soft and mellow quality of Roshanji's music. His songs were never sung forcefully and if the film's story demanded it, as was the case in *Chitralekha*, he turned to classical music. In the 1990s, when I recorded the first *Shraddhanjali* album, I included a tribute to Rafi Sahib and sang Roshanji's 'Mann re tu kaahe na dheer dhare.'

NMK: What did you think of his *qawali*s?

LM: Excellent! 'Naa to kaaravaan ki talaash hai' in *Barsaat ki Raat* and Asha's 'Nigahein milaane ko ji chahata hai' from *Dil Hi to Hai* were beautiful. His romantic songs had a soothing quality. Roshanji created an exceptional mood in his music. He had a great sense of humour. And was a terrific mimic and danced very well — like his grandson Hrithik!

NMK: When you speak of Roshanji's 'madhur' musical style, so evident in his songs, was this sweetness part of his personality? Do you think there is a link between artists and their work?

LM: Most definitely. An artist's personality is visible in his or her art.

NMK: What aspect of your personality is present in your singing?

LM: *[long pause]* My concentration. I give full attention to a song. When I sing, I forget everything else. I apply my mind to making it better.

NMK: Your focus and concentration are indeed formidable. I don't know many people who listen so attentively and are as alert as you.

LM: *[smiles]*

NMK: I know you were very close to Madan Mohanji. Could you say something about how your friendship started?

LM: When Ghulam Haider Sahib wanted me to sing in *Shaheed*, and it hadn't worked out, he still went ahead and recorded a duet which was going to be mimed in *Shaheed* by actors playing a brother and sister. Madan Bhaiya sang this duet with me, but it was ultimately deleted from the film and never released on disc. However, Madan Bhaiya liked my voice and said: 'I am composing music for a film and you must sing for me.' I said: 'Very well.'

In the meantime someone came and told me Madan Bhaiya had spoken against me. I don't know what came over me, but I refused to sing for him. I never went to the recording. He was hurt and a few days later he came over to see me and said: 'Why did you do this to me?' So I asked him why he had spoken ill of me and he assured me he hadn't. 'Are you crazy? We sang a duet as brother and sister, so I am like a brother to you. On *rakhi* you will have to come and see me.' And so Madan Bhaiya became my *rakhi* brother.

While we were rehearsing, Madan Bhaiya would keep singing and then say: 'Take whatever sounds right to you.' Taken aback, I would react: 'How is it possible, Madan Bhaiya? *[laughs]* Teach me the whole song from start to finish in the way you want me to record it.'

Sometimes he hummed a long musical phrase *[she hums]*. I had to ask him to stop: 'Madan Bhaiya, how long is this *taan*?' He just wouldn't stop. He would finally say: 'All right, I'll sing it properly for you.' Then he would teach me the song — from start to finish. He was a fine music director. No one wrote film *ghazals* like Madan Mohan. Many have tried and are still trying, but no one has succeeded.

NMK: Once he became your *rakhi* brother, how did your relationship change?

LM: We were like one family. I spent days with him. He cooked very well, and mutton cooked by his hand was delicious. He often invited me over for a meal. One day he told me: 'Beta [child] I'm going to Punjab and bringing back a sister-in-law for you.' Then he showed me a photograph of his future wife and asked: 'How do you like her? If you like her then I'll marry her, if you don't, I won't.' I said: 'What are you saying?' *[laughs]*

In 1952, he got married to Sheila Dhingra and came back to Bombay. I attended a small party he held to celebrate his wedding. He didn't invite many guests, but Naushad Sahib, Ghulam Mohammed Sahib, and just a few other composers were there. Madan Bhaiya made me sit next to him and treated me as a family member, and together we welcomed the guests. He also made sure I ate well.

NMK: I believe you enjoy cooking very much. Who taught you?

LM: It was my maternal grandmother and mother who taught me how to cook. I started cooking when I was very young and often made lunch and dinner at home. In later years, Mrs. Bhalji Pendharkar, whom we called Bakula Mausi, taught me how to cook some dishes. She was a dear and close family friend. I called her 'Ma.' I was very close to her and often stayed with her. She used to wash my hair and taught me how to make *pulao* and mutton. And many vegetarian dishes too. Mrs. Majrooh Sultanpuri showed me how to make *pasanda* and chicken curry.

I cook quickly and the kitchen is always left neat and tidy after I have finished. The pleasure of cooking isn't in cooking, but seeing people enjoy the meal and say they have liked what I made for them — that makes me happy. Earlier, when I used to spend time in London, I always used to cook there.

NMK: And what about your love for photography?

LM: That started in 1946. I was on an outdoor shoot and took a picture of someone who was standing by a river. I became intrigued by photography. I told Madhavrao Shinde, the film editor, about my interest and he taught me the basics: how to load film and the kind of camera I should buy.

The first stills camera I ever owned was a Rolleiflex. I bought it for 1200 rupees.

NMK: Did you enjoy photographing landscapes?

LM: I couldn't really. Because every time I stepped out of the car to take a picture, someone or other would recognise me and start talking to me. Soon a crowd would gather and I could barely see the landscape beyond the wall of fans. So no more landscapes! *[both laugh]*

I took many pictures of my family, and when I travelled abroad as well. Few people outside India recognised or bothered me in the early days. Now there's digital photography. It doesn't interest me.

NMK: What kind of things do you enjoy doing in your free time?

With Madan Mohan

LM: This may sound strange but when I used to visit America on holiday, I loved spending time in Las Vegas. It's an exciting city. I really enjoyed playing the slot machines. *[both laugh]* I never played roulette or cards — but I used to spend the whole night at a slot machine. I was very lucky and won many times. Meena and Usha and sometimes my nieces and nephews would accompany me. I would drink Coca-Cola all through the night and play. The next morning, we would have breakfast: fried eggs and a glass of milk. This was our Las Vegas routine. These little escapes were enjoyable and relaxing.

NMK: You are a most unpredictable person! The image frequently projected of you is quite different from the real Lata Mangeshkar! You are so open to learning and have such a zest for life. There is also your great interest in cricket.

LM: The first Test match I saw was with my sister Meena at the Brabourne Stadium in Bombay in 1945 or maybe 1946 — it was a match between Australia and India. We sat in the stands. The Indian captain was Vijay Merchant and the Australian captain, Lindsey Hassett.

My love for cricket dates back to the time when Baba had his theatre company in the '30s and early '40s. We had a cricket team and the actors and workers played together. Vijay Samuel Hazare, the famous cricketer, would come to see my father when we were touring with the theatre troupe. Hazare led India to win the first ever Test match in 1951-52 against England.

So we grew up with cricket. My mother loved it too. Hridaynath and Meena are great cricket experts. Whenever there was a five-day Test match, I would take a break from recording and the whole family would go together.

It was a picnic for us, a family day out. We'd take something to eat and thoroughly enjoy the game.

In those days, cricket fans were the quiet sort, not like now! Many royal families came to watch too. They sat in the pavilions, and the middle and lower middle classes sat in the stands.

This was the time when there was no television and we could only follow the match on the radio. There were many players I liked and have seen play, including Gary Sobers and Rohan Kanhai who were in the West Indies team; Richie Benaud, Ray Lindwall, Alan Davidson and Neil Harvey from Australia. And from India, Mushtaq Ali, Vinoo Mankad, Vijay Merchant, Mansoor Ali Khan Pataudi, Sunil Gavaskar and Sachin Tendulkar. I was too young to see C.K. Nayudu play.

I even have a signed photograph of Don Bradman. He wrote: 'To Lata!' When I visited London, I went to Lord's and the Oval. I once watched a Test Match between Pakistan and England at the Oval. But as time passed, I began watching cricket on television.

NMK: I am curious to know if you have friends among the cricketers?

LM: Vijay Hazare was a family friend. I have also been close to Vinoo Mankad, Bhishen Singh Bedi, Sunil Gavaskar, Kapil Dev and Sachin Tendulkar.

NMK: It is rumoured you have a permanent gallery reserved for you at Lord's '...where she enjoys watching her favourite game.' Is it true?

LM: No! It's not true. *[laughs]* I sit in the stands like any other cricket fan.

NMK: Coming back to your work. You said you believed words are the most important aspect of a song. Did the lyricists attend the recording sessions? Did they change any words before the take?

LM: I never needed to ask Sahir Sahib, Majrooh Sahib or Shailendraji to change a single word. With other songwriters I sometimes insisted on a word change. I do not like vulgar words or lines with double meanings. I remember arguing with Hasrat Jaipuri over 'Main kaa karun Ram mujhe buddha mil gayaa.' The words really irritated me. I found them vulgar. But Raj Kapoor explained the song situation in *Sangam*. He said the wife is teasing her husband and it's a humoristic song. He also said it was very much in the style of Punjabi folk songs in which a husband is asked to buy something for his wife and instead of buying what she wants, he brings back a cabbage or something else. So I sang the song, but I chose not to see *Sangam*. I also remember refusing to sing 'Main bahaaron ki natkhat raani,' a song Hasrat Jaipuri had written for *Boot Polish*.

I had frequent arguments with Jaikishan on the subject of vulgar lyrics. He often tried to persuade me to set aside my objections. Gradually I gained the reputation of not singing 'cheap' songs. So people stopped approaching me with a certain kind of cabaret number or songs with double meanings.

NMK: I read an interview with Hasrat Jaipuri in which he also mentioned the fact you didn't like the words of the *Boot Polish* song.

There were so many Muslim poets and songwriters who wrote in Urdu. Do you feel Urdu is particularly well suited to emotions and lyrics?

LM: Urdu and Hindi poetry was popular at one time and the songs were often a mix of the two. Of course Urdu has been used a lot in film songs. But I believe every language is expressive. We have good lyricists who write in Marathi and Bengali too. You get a flavour of culture in songs of all languages. I am sure you know many lovely songs in English.

NMK: Absolutely. The songs of Bob Dylan and the Beatles are real poetry. But what makes a film song poetic for you?

LM: The choice of words and whether thoughts and feelings have been suitably expressed. In a love song, you ask if emotions are poetically described. But the most important thing is that the song is right for the filmic situation in which it appears.

Many music directors first compose the tune and lyrics are then written on that tune. I think it's difficult to make words fit music. Majrooh Sahib and Shailendraji had great talent in doing this. Take 'Aaja re pardesi,' Salil Chowdhury composed the tune and then Shailendraji wrote the words. I once sang a Bengali non-film romantic song called 'Naa jeyo naa.' Non-film songs are very popular in Bengal and are usually released around Durga Pooja and this is one such song. On the same metre of 'Naa jeyo naa,' Shailendraji wrote 'O sajanaa… barkhaa bahaar aayi' for the film *Parakh*. Shailendraji's songs were excellent. He wrote wonderfully in Hindi and equally well in Urdu. Though he was essentially a Hindi poet, he combined Hindi and Urdu with great skill.

I liked Shakeel Badayuni's poetry very much. He wrote sweet songs, using beautifully expressive words, as did Sahir Saab, Raja Mehdi Ali Khan and Rajinder Krishenji.

Pradeepji could write lyrics, compose music and sing too. He was a unique kind of man and his poetry was different. 'Ae mere watan ke logon,' one of Pradeepji's songs, composed by C. Ramchandra, is still extremely popular. As you know it wasn't composed for a film, but whenever I perform in public, people still ask me to sing it.

Jaan Nisar Akhtar wrote wonderfully. His songs perfectly suited the filmic situation. His son, Javed Akhtar, is also a good lyricist. He is an extremely witty man and great

With the celebrated Sachin Tendulkar, who calls Lata Mangeshkar 'Ma.'

company. We get along very well and always have a good laugh when we meet. In fact, there is no end to our laughter.

NMK: And Gulzar Sahib?

LM: Gulzar Sahib directed *Lekin*, a film produced by Hridaynath. When I hear some of the *Lekin* songs, especially 'Surmai shaam is tarah aaye,' sung by Suresh Wadkar, my eyes are moist. Suresh Wadkar is a very good singer and sings classical music too. He has sung very often for Hridaynath's albums and has a music school for children where he teaches. He has sung in many films, including *Prem Rog* and *Ram Teri Ganga Maili*. Gulzar Sahib's fine thoughts bring tears to my eyes. Sometimes when I am sitting alone, I think of a couplet from 'Surmai shaam is tarah aaye:'

Din ka jo bhi pehar guzarta hai
Koi ehsaan sa utarta hai

Every moment that passes in a day
Is like the bestowing of a favour

These lines seem true about life too. That's why I like Gulzarji's poetry very much. It is quite modern.

NMK: Can you tell me if you think lyrics dictate the setting of the song? For example, 'Ye wadiya ye fizaayen bula rahi hain tumhen' [These valleys, this nature calls out to you] has to be filmed in a valley with nature surrounding the hero and heroine. Do you think this matching of words and location is limiting for a filmmaker?

LM: Not really. Most directors predetermine the moment when the song will occur. They set the scene for the song. The scene then sets off the imagination of the lyricist and the composer. Nowadays there aren't many real situations for songs, so people just get up and dance!

NMK: That's another way of explaining the 'item' number! A song with no particular narrative reason to exist but merely added into the film to stretch an already paper-thin story. Can you give me an example of a song expressing emotion and at the same time advancing the narrative?

LM: There are many examples. Take 'Jo humne daastan apni sunaayi aap kyun roye' in *Woh Kaun Thi*, and 'O jaane waalon jaao na ghar apna chhod ke' in *Mother India* and 'Jab pyaar kiya to darna kya' in *Mughal-e-Azam* — these songs advance the narrative like dialogue.

NMK: Perfect examples. When Anarkali sings 'Jab pyaar kiya to darna kya,' the song is a challenge addressed to Emperor Akbar, creating a dramatic turn in the story. The power of the scene is enhanced by the way you sing the song. Anarkali's anger and defiance comes through in your voice. It's a musical declaration of war!
You say you hated acting as a young girl but I think you are an amazing actress. I often wonder if it's ever possible to separate the strong element of 'performance' in your singing from the overall acting abilities of the actress who mimes your songs? Is it her acting or your voice that gives the emotion to the scene? Impossible to separate!

LM: I can't say much about that. But I remember Meena Kumariji once told me, when I was singing for her, she didn't need to act!

At Famous in Tardeo. 1960s.

Singing with emotion is absolutely vital. For example in *Satyam Shivam Sundaram,* I sang two versions of 'Yashomati maiya' — the first was picturised on Padmini Kolhapure who plays the young Roopa, and the second is mimed by Zeenat Aman, the adult Roopa. I tried to make sure the expressions were different in order to suggest the age of the characters and differentiate between a young girl's emotions and a young woman's.

One of the most difficult emotions to express in a song is that of a mother. In *Mother India*, the song 'O mere laal aaja' was very difficult because the situation in the film was so complicated. Here is this son running away from the law and his mother implores him to stop through her song. There are so many emotions going through her mind.

Although I am not a mother myself, I have been a mother and father to my siblings. When my father died, I took on the responsibility of the family and understood from a very early age what nurturing meant. So, when I sing a song for a mother, I know her feelings — the mix of unconditional love and deep responsibility.

NMK: For someone who has always been so responsible, you have the most infectious laugh. It has an innocent, childlike quality. I get the feeling it's the one thing that hasn't changed at all since you were a child — your laugh.

LM: You may be right. *[smiles]*

NMK: Is it important to laugh?

LM: Yes, very. You stay alive if you laugh. There is no point in being morose or too philosophical. If I sat in front of you with a long face, you'd get bored. We remain human if we laugh. I always think: happiness is for sharing with the world and sorrow is for keeping to yourself.

There are no guarantees in life. I believe everything you get is a favour granted by God. Whatever we have is thanks to Him. Our lives are entirely in God's hands. Whatever people do in life is because God has willed it. It is God who believed you should write this book. So you will write it and go.

NMK: I hope we're not talking about an imminent and final departure?

LM: *[laughs]* I hope not!

NMK: When we were talking of *Mughal-e-Azam*, I was reminded of a bit of trivia I read on the Net. It said in order to create the reverb in 'Jab pyaar kiya to darna kya,' Naushad Sahib got you to record the song in a studio bathroom. Is this true?

LM: *[irritated]* How can people think such things? Record in a studio bathroom? The person who has written that has clearly never been inside a studio bathroom!

I was standing at the mic in Mehboob Recording Studio when I sang the song. The chorus singers and I were the only ones in the otherwise empty recording hall. Naushad Sahib asked me to sing the main line a number of times, creating a gap or pause in between. 'Pyaar kiya to darna kya...' pause and then again 'Jab pyaar kiya to darna kya...' This line was then layered onto the track to create an echo effect – as if many voices were singing it. Record in a studio bathroom, if you please!

NMK: There is quite a lot of misinformation about the way you all worked. And sadly these stories spread as if they were true. It's a bit irritating. What kinds of things make you angry?

LM: I am usually quite patient. But when I hear anyone saying something that I know to be a lie, I get angry. I might not let on and usually go quiet, but inside I am angry when people lie. I can't say I'm a great reader of character but I can tell when someone is genuine or not. I may not get it 100 per cent right, maybe 75 per cent.

Another thing that really makes me angry is when I hear someone sing out of tune. I can't stand it! *[both laugh]*

NMK: I wanted to ask you again about Majrooh Sultanpuri. How would you describe his skills?

LM: Majrooh Sahib has written all kinds of lyrics. He has written in *thumri* style and *ghazal*s too. He was an extremely good poet and excellent songwriter. But I will say that his personal nobility far excelled his exquisite poetry. He was a man of God. I am very fond of his whole family and they have great affection for me. We saw each other very often.

When Majrooh Sahib had a severe attack of pneumonia and was admitted into hospital, I wasn't in Bombay at the time and my nephew, Adinath, visited him. He knew he was dying and even told Adinath he would not last long. Majrooh Sahib passed away on 24th May, 2000. He was a fine human being.

[Lataji pauses and folds her hands in a namaskar*]*

I can only bow humbly before these great people. Sahir Sahib, Majrooh Sahib, Shailendraji, Rajinder Krishen, Shakeel Badayuni, Hasrat Jaipuri, Raja Mehdi Ali Khan,

Kaifi Azmi, Kavi Pradeep — when this generation of lyricists and composers, including Anil Biswas, Naushad Sahib, Shyam Sundar, Madan Mohan, Shankar-Jaikishan, Roshan, Hemant Kumar, Jaidev, Salil Chowdhury, S.D. Burman, R.D. Burman, Sajjad Hussain, Ghulam Mohammed, C. Ramchandra, N. Datta, K. Datta, Sudhir Phadke and Vasant Desai passed away, their understanding of music ended with them. Each one of them had the stamp of an artist with individual gift and style.

Their passing has marked the end of an extraordinary era of film music.

NMK: I am sure millions of people would agree with you. Great people in music and in the political life of India have passed away. I believe tears came to Pandit Nehru's eyes when you sang 'Ae mere watan ke logon' [O people of my country]. When was this?

LM: Following the Chinese attack on India in 1962, Pradeepji wrote this song and I sang it for the first time in Delhi on Republic Day on 26th January, 1963. C. Ramchandra conducted the few musicians who were performing on stage with me. That year, many stars and music directors from Bombay were in Delhi, including Dilip Kumar, Raj Kapoor, Naushad Ali, Shankar-Jaikishan and Madan Mohan. Once I finished singing I sat down behind the stage and asked for a coffee. Mehboob Sahib came rushing to me and said: 'Lata! Where is Lata? Panditji is calling you.' I followed him outside and when Panditji saw me, he stood up. Indiraji and many leading politicians were there too. Mehboob Sahib introduced me saying: 'This is Lata Mangeshkar.' He said: 'Beta, tum ne aaj mujhe rula diya [Child, you have brought tears to my eyes today]. I am going home now. Come and have tea with me.'

We all then went to have tea at Teen Murti Bhavan where the Prime Minister was living. I am not very pushy, so I stood in a corner when Mrs. Indira Gandhi came over to me and said: 'You're here? Please wait. Don't move. I want to introduce two fans to you. They love your songs.' She returned with her young sons, Rajiv and Sanjay. At that moment, Panditji asked after me: 'Where is the lady who sang?' So I went across the room and stood near him. He turned to me and said: 'Will you sing it again?' 'I won't sing now,' I replied politely.

Photographs were taken of us and were printed everywhere.

NMK: Did you meet Panditji again?

LM: Yes. He came to Bombay to attend a charity show. I believe it was sometime in early 1964. The event was held at the Brabourne Stadium, the Bombay cricket grounds near

Churchgate and I sang the *Arzoo* song 'Aji rooth kar ab kahan jaiyega.' When I was on the stage, I received a message from Panditji asking me to sing 'Ae mere watan ke logon.' So I sang it.

Panditji was quite unwell in those days and didn't stay very long. He was sitting in his car with his sister Vijayalakshmi Pandit. Ram Kamlani, the brother of comedian Gope, rushed to me and said: 'Lata, where are you? Panditji is calling you.'

So we went to Panditji's car. He rolled down the window and held my hand and said: 'I came to hear you sing "Ae mere watan ke logon." I am glad I have heard you sing.' He drove away soon after we talked.

Panditji was always so affectionate. I am honoured to have met him. Mrs. Gandhi was very warm with me too. I was in Kolhapur on 27 May, 1964 when I heard Panditji was no more. It was a sad day.

A day later, Mai called and told me Mehboob Sahib had passed away. I immediately sent a telegram to his wife Sardar Akhtar.

NMK: It must have been a very sad time. Where were you when you heard that Mahatma Gandhi had been assassinated?

LM: There was a function held on Friday, 30 January, 1948 at Filmistan in Goregaon to celebrate the Silver Jubilee of the film *Shehnai*. Many guests were there, including Madan Mohan's father, Rai Bahadur Chunilal, the owner of Filmistan. That day I happened to be rehearsing in one of the rooms and had to leave early because I had other work to do. I went to Goregaon station to board the train and noticed the carriage was completely empty. Then someone told me Gandhiji had been assassinated.

Riots broke out everywhere. I sat in the train compartment alone. I was terrified. I remember crying.

NMK: Did you ever meet Gandhiji?

LM: No, but I heard him speak at a public gathering at Shivaji Park and at Chowpatty in Bombay in the early 1940s. He made a great impression on us and on everyone who was there. We all had tremendous respect for Gandhiji and for Jai Prakash Narayan too. But I had no interest in politics then nor do politics interest me now.

With Pandit Nehru.

With former Prime Minister Indira Gandhi.

NMK: Do you remember where you were on 15th August, 1947 — Independence day?

LM: We were at home and in the evening, we all went out to see the lights. There was much rejoicing in the streets and a great feeling of happiness. It was a big day.

NMK: I am curious about whether the British, when they were in India, were at all interested in Indian cinema? Or film music? Do you remember any British officials visiting the studios where you worked?

LM: They may have come to see the studios' bosses, but they certainly didn't come to see me! I don't remember seeing a single British person at any recording session. The only foreigner I met in the 1940s was Kamal Amrohi Sahib's cameraman who was working on *Mahal*. I think he was British.

NMK: Actually he was German. You're thinking of Joseph Wirsching. With Hitler's rise in the 1930s, some German film technicians left the famous UFA studios and worked in India with Himanshu Rai. So cameraman Joseph Wirsching who shot *Mahal* was working at Bombay Talkies, producers of *Mahal.* He died during the making of *Pakeezah,* though he had photographed most of the film. The great strength of the film industry is how it has always welcomed people of all communities, irrespective of class and creed. Rafi Sahib and you have recorded hundreds of love duets, and no one has ever remarked in a negative way about you being a Hindu and he being a Muslim. Hindus and Muslims have always worked together in cinema without any sense of divide. Was that your experience?

LM: Yes, we all worked together – there were Hindu and Muslim music directors, lyricists and singers. Sometimes we discussed why Hindus and Muslims fought one another. We are the same. We are the same colour and the same race. So why? Naushad Sahib considered me like his younger sister; he never saw me as different. I spent a lot of time with Majrooh Sahib and his family; I never thought of them as different. We were never divided on religious grounds. We never felt any tension between us because some were Hindu and others Muslim. Yet, there was a lot of communal tension around us in those early days.

In 1946, terrible riots broke out in Bombay. We were so worried, to the extent that Mai decided to take us all to Kolhapur where we stayed in Master Vinayak's house. But it wasn't long before we returned to Bombay.

For me there is no difference between Hindu and Muslim. I didn't see the difference then nor do I see it now. I see the person. If I don't like a person, I just don't like him or her. But my likes and dislikes have nothing to do with them being Hindu, Muslim, Sikh or Christian.

NMK: Your respect for different faiths shows in your singing. A sense of spirituality is present whether you are singing a *bhajan* or a *naat.*

LM: It is the words of a *naat*, *bhajan* or *kirtan* that inspire me. The mood of the song is different. I haven't sung *qawali*s addressed to Allah like the traditional *qawali*. If you remember the *qawali* I sang with Shamshad Begum, 'Teri mehfil mein kismat azamaa kar hum bhi dekhenge,' *in Mughal-e-Azam*; this was a romantic *qawali*.

NMK: I am curious to know when you visited Europe for the first time.

LM: In 1967. On my way to Canada, I stopped in London for two days and stayed with Asha's son, Hemant, who was studying flying there. He was staying with Pratap Barot, director Chandra Barot's elder brother.

I was visiting Canada to see Nalini Mhatre, a very close friend of mine. She was a psychiatrist. I met her in 1949 at St. Xavier's where she was studying. I was singing at a music programme held at the college and my sister Meena became friends with Nalini. Later she became a friend of mine. In 1958, she migrated to Canada to join her two brothers who had settled in Kingston. She had a third brother who lived in America.

NMK: It may sound silly to say this but it's surprising to hear one of your closest friends was a psychiatrist.

LM: I like the idea of meeting people outside of films. Nalini used to pull my leg and say I needed her help. I jokingly told her: 'There's nothing wrong with me. I am not in the least bit crazy!' Nalini was unmarried and had a house in Kingston. When I first visited her in October 1967, she showed me around Toronto. It was freezing and there was wet snow everywhere. I spent two weeks with her and sometime during that time, she heard her mother had passed away.

From Canada I flew back to London. I visited a few places, including the British Museum. I remember eating a sandwich somewhere and falling very ill. I had food poisoning. I was so unwell and couldn't do any more sightseeing. It was difficult for me. I didn't speak English fluently so I headed back to Bombay as soon as possible. For weeks after my return I continued to be unwell.

Nalini passed away in April 1996. She died of cancer. I was very upset and sad when I heard the news. She was one of my dearest and closest friends.

NMK: I read somewhere you once said if you were born again, you would prefer not to be a woman. Why is that?

LM: Now I would say I prefer not to be reborn at all. If God wills it, that's another matter. Who knows what form I will take. That's if I am reborn. But I prefer not to be.

NMK: Maybe you just think that today, and if you were in a place where you felt happy or were with people who made you happy, you might feel differently.

LM: *[laughs]*

NMK: Coming back to music, what about the generation of composers from the '60s?

LM: Whether you consider them part of the old or new generation, Laxmikant-Pyarelal, Ravindra Jain and R.D. Burman were among the leading composers by the 1970s.

R.D. Burman was of course Burmanda's son but he developed his own style which was different from his father's. He was influenced by Western music and was very fond of it. He blended Western and Indian musical styles in his songs, and the results were very good. Think of the duets 'O haseena zulfonwali' or 'Aaja aaja main hoon pyaar tera' from *Teesri Manzil* and 'Piya tu ab to aaja' from *Caravan.*

R.D. was a music director who composed tunes according to an artist's ability. The songs he composed for Asha were meant just for her and suited her voice. You will find the songs he wrote for me are completely different. They sound as though they were composed uniquely for Lata.

NMK: R.D. Burman's music is even more popular today than ever before. Why do you think this has happened?

LM: People have understood what a great music director he was. He set trends that many copy today. Dance numbers are so popular now — perhaps that's why people think of R.D. Burman. He composed so many dance numbers but no one can match the ones he wrote.

NMK: He composed great numbers for Shammi Kapoor's and Helen's films, and their youthful style of dancing connects to this generation. In fact, I think Shammiji was a key influence on the 1990s heroes especially evident in the early films of the Khan stars. But I am sure you will agree the 1980s music wasn't any good?

LM: I think the 1980s music isn't as weak as the music today! *[laughs]*

Nalini Mhatre was a psychiatrist and a close friend who lived in Canada. Lata Mangeshkar was deeply upset when she passed away in 1996.

NMK: Of course! I am forgetting Laxmikant-Pyarelal's and R.D. Burman's output! Laxmikant-Pyarelal were the top composers till the early 1990s. What distinguishes their work for you?

LM: Laxmikant-Pyarelal followed Shankar-Jaikishan to a great extent — particularly in their orchestration. Pyarelal's musical arrangement was distinctive and good. He thought a lot about what he composed. The music accompanying the lyrics was usually fantastic. I believe if you impose a huge orchestral sound on a song, then the words become less important and the orchestra takes over. I personally don't like that. The early music directors composed just enough music to support the lyrics, not to drown them.

I always say: 'In the early days, the orchestra played music to give us singers a rest. Now we sing in order to give the orchestra a rest!' *[both laugh]*

NMK: I hear you helped Laxmikant-Pyarelal at the start of their career?

LM: In the 1960s, Hridaynath had set up the Sureel Bala Kendra and through this music centre, he organised programmes all over Maharashtra. My sisters Meena and Usha, along with many gifted children, including young Laxmikant and Pyarelal performed in these shows. That's how we got to know them. Laxmikant was about ten and played the mandolin and his brother, Shashikant, played the *tabla*.

The first time I saw Laxmikant was thanks to K.L. Saigal's brother, Mahendra Saigal who took me to a concert in Bombay because he wanted me to hear Laxmikant play the mandolin. He said he was very good and I should help the young musician find work.

When I first met Pyarelal, he was about ten years old and played the violin. His father, Pandit Ramprasad Sharma, was a musician who played the trumpet and also the violin. He taught Pyarelal when he was five. I believe Pyarelal met Laxmikant at a concert organised by Hridaynath in which Meena sang too.

NMK: Pandit Ramprasad Sharma can be heard playing the trumpet in the background of that famous Rafi Sahib song, 'Suhaani raat dhal chuki' in *Dulari.* And Pyarelal played the violin in the unusual 'Eena meena deeka' by C. Ramchandra in *Aasha*.

I believe at one point Pyarelal continued studying the violin and was taught by a Goan arranger/musician called Anthony Gonsalves whose name was borrowed by Amitabh Bachchan in Manmohan Desai's *Amar Akbar Anthony.* When Laxmikant and Pyarelal were older, did you continue helping them?

LM: I recommended them to Shankar-Jaikishan and Ghulam Mohammed Sahib and from the 1950s, they worked as musicians for these composers. They played the mandolin and violin in many songs, including those of Naushad Sahib and Madan Mohanji. They later became assistants to Kalyanji-Anandji for many years, and worked on films like *Himalay ki Godh Mein*. Did you know Kalyanji-Anandji were my neighbours? They lived just across the road from me. They have composed so many hits. I was very sad when Kalyanji passed away.

I sang the greatest number of songs with Laxmikant-Pyarelal and most of these were very popular. They collaborated closely with lyricist Anand Bakshi who came to Bombay hoping to be a playback singer. In fact, Anand Bakshi and I sang the duet 'Baghon mein bahaar ayi' in *Mome ki Gudiya*. He sometimes composed tunes and gave them to Laxmikant-Pyarelal. They worked with many top directors, including Raj Kapoor, Manmohan Desai and Subhash Ghai. And composed music for Yash Chopra's *Daag*.

NMK: You've sung some wonderful songs by Laxmikant-Pyarelal and these were nearly all back-to-back hits. I am thinking of the *Milan* duet 'Sawan ka mahina pawan kare shor' with Mukeshji. Was it fun to record? In the scene Sunil Dutt is teaching Nutan the song.

LM: Mukesh Bhaiya and I did laugh because he thought it was amusing to be teaching me how to sing.

NMK: Anand Bakshi, among others, wrote quite a few songs that work like conversation. I am reminded of 'Achcha to hum chalte hain' in *Aan Milo Sajna* and the 'Hum tum ek kamre mein bandh ho' in *Bobby*. Are such songs rendered in a different way?

LM: Such songs are interesting for both my co-singer and me. You have to have a different kind of expression when singing this kind of duet, and make it sound like two people talking to one another. It's almost dialogue. But every word is spoken in tune and follows the melody. In the *Bobby* song it was important to make it sound very youthful because the hero and heroine are teenagers and so 'Hum tum ek kamre' had to sound youthful.

The conversation duets were very popular. Kishoreda and I sang 'Achcha to hum chalte hain' as we were leaving the stage during a *Filmfare* awards night. The audience just loved it.

NMK: Khayyam Sahib has often talked about the purity of your voice and your flawless Urdu diction.

LM: I haven't sung many songs by Khayyam Sahib, but have liked the ones I did sing. He has a distinctive style. When he explains a song, he points out every little detail. He is very particular about getting the poetry right. He believes the words must be just right. He's given to suspicions: 'Will we manage the song? What will happen if we get it wrong? It should be like this, but what if it isn't? Who's that man hanging about? What does he want? Will he steal my tune?' Khayyam Sahib has an unusual manner!

He's so good-hearted and always very affectionate towards me. I sang his 'Apne aap raaton mein' and 'Aap yun faaslon se guzarte rehe' for a small film called *Shankar Hussain.* I don't think the film was successful but these were fine songs.

NMK: People have loved your 'Ae dil-e-nadaan' from *Razia Sultan,* another Khayyam Sahib composition with lyrics by Jaan Nisar Akhtar. Khayyam Sahib once said you had recorded it in a single take.

LM: I don't remember. But I know the recording at Mehboob Studio didn't take long. Khayyam Sahib was never fully satisfied with any song recording and always said: 'We can do better.' Kamal Amrohi Sahib who directed *Razia Sultan* also knew the kind of emotions his songs should express.

NMK: I believe you were very angry to discover the *Razia Sultan* song had been pirated.

LM: That's right. I went into a saree shop in America — I don't recall which city — and heard 'Ae dil-e-nadaan' in a store. Of course it was disheartening to hear it playing in a public place even before the record had been released. I told Kamal Amrohi

Lata Mangeshkar was a guide and mentor to the composing-duo, Laxmikant-Pyarelal who became top music directors of Hindi cinema.

Sahib about it but there was nothing he could do. This didn't happen very often but I remember this incident.

NMK: What about the music of Rajesh Roshan?

LM: His songs were very popular particularly in the '80s and '90s. His style of composition wasn't like his father's [Roshan Lal] but his work was much appreciated. I had a good relationship with Chitragupt too and have recorded many of his songs. His sons, Anand-Milind, are good composers. And there's Jatin-Lalit. Their music for *Dilwale Dulhania Le Jayenge* was so popular. I haven't sung a lot for Anu Malik — I sang for his *Radha ka Sangam* and a few other films. I like Shankar-Ehsaan-Loy's music.

NMK: What do you think of the new generation of singers? And A.R. Rahman?

LM: Sonu Nigam, Udit Narayan, Alka Yagnik, P. Sushila, Sunidhi Chauhan and Kavitha Krishnamurthy are good singers. But I believe Kavitha Krishnamurthy doesn't sing much any more.

A.R. Rahman is now acclaimed all round the world and really deserved the Oscars he received. This is the first time the world has recognised and honoured Indian film music in this manner. I am proud of Rahman. He has a unique sound, originality, and has developed a style all his own. A.R. Rahman's songs are simple and have effective orchestration. He is an excellent arranger and technician. He understands sound mixing perfectly and sings well too. And his music has worked well in films like *Lagaan* and *Rang de Basanti* and more recently *Slumdog Millionaire*. The lyricist, Prasoon Joshi, who wrote the songs in *Rang De Basanti* writes well.

I remember Rahman sent me a tape of the song 'Jia jale' for *Dil Se* sung in his own voice. Then I went to his studio in Chennai. And he said I should just sing into the mic. I started rehearsing then realised he was recording the rehearsals. He always gives me the freedom to sing an *alaap* the way I feel like. Rahman keeps recording whatever I sing, even during rehearsals and edits it all together. This was a new experience for me. He has a different way of working. There's never any tension when recording in his studio in Chennai. I am relaxed and like working with him.

NMK: Nusrat Fateh Ali Khan is loved around the world. Was there ever any plan to collaborate together?

LM: The first time we met in Bombay, we didn't talk much. Not long before he passed away, he came to Bombay and I invited him home for dinner. He composed music for *Kachche Dhaage* and said he was leaving for London and if I could please record the songs. I sang the solo 'Tere bin nahin jeena.' Nusrat Sahib was a good man.

NMK: The music for *Veer Zaara* has a very interesting history. Could you recount what actually happened?

LM: Madan Mohanji had written about two hundred songs that were never recorded. And Yashji knew about this material. When he started *Veer Zaara,* Yashji decided to use some of Madan Bhaiya's music and thought why not ask Sanjeev Kohli, Madan Mohan's son, to work on the idea? Sanjeev went through all the old tapes and selected some tunes and played them to Yashji. Together they decided on what would work best for the film, and then we all went into the recording studio. It was nice working on Madan Bhaiya's tunes again. Sanjeev cannot sing the song to explain the tune, but has a great ear for music. He is a perfectionist and understood exactly how to arrange the score with the right instrumentation and orchestration. Javed Akhtar Sahib wrote the lyrics. Sanjeev worked very hard and the music turned out very well.

NMK: The film's songs are indeed memorable. What is your brother's contribution to the world of film music?

LM: To speak of my brother and sisters is awkward. I have sung for many non-film albums composed by my brother: the devotional songs of Meerabai, the *Bhagvad Gita*, and *ghazal*s by Ghalib. I'm not saying this because he is my brother, but I think his music for *Lekin* is so unusual — it was a little classical and light music and suited the film's story very well. He has composed music for a few other films, but I believe his songs in *Lekin* and *Maya Memsaab* will always be regarded as somewhat different.

NMK: Isn't there a lot of Rajasthani folk music in *Lekin*?

LM: Not in all the songs, but 'Kesariya balama' is in Rajasthani. It's a popular folk tune and people still sing it in Rajasthan.Another music composer and singer who has created wonderful music in the tradition of Assamese folk music is Bhupen Hazarika. His songs are excellent and I have sung many of his compositions. I remember one of his lovely songs that described the beauty of Assam.

NMK: Is there a difference when you sing for a composer who also happens to be your brother?

LM: To tell you the truth, I am always afraid I'll get it wrong. Hridaynath's music is difficult and I know I must sing the songs exactly the way he wants them sung. He composes music on the lyrics and not the other way round. He was Ustaad Amir Khan's disciple. We don't argue at all, but if I sing even slightly off key or make a mistake, Hridaynath will immediately stop the recording and say: 'You are singing in front of ten people here but one day this song will be heard by a million. Didi, you have a big name and you can't get it wrong.'

The whole family has grown up with this feeling that above all we can't tarnish our father's name in music.

Hridaynath is influenced by my father's music. Baba wrote music for the many plays that he produced. In fact, the *Lekin* song 'Main ek sadi se baithi hoon' is based on a composition by Baba.

My brother pays most attention to the lyrics and makes sure they work in the film. Naushad Sahib believed in the same principle. They researched the story background thoroughly — and if the film is set in a village, they composed folk-style music to avoid an orchestral sound.

NMK: So you're saying, not only must the song words be appropriate to the narrative, but also the tunes must be authentic to the world depicted.

LM: Yes, they should flow with the story of the film. Hridaynath always writes music matching the mood of the words. When we were recording Meerabai's *bhajans*, he first wrote a storyline for this non-film album. Meera is singing in a temple. She leaves her home. She becomes an ascetic and so on. He created a story and then composed the music. The album 'Chala Vaahi Des,' was released in 1974. It was greatly appreciated by Gulzar Sahib and inspired him to eventually make the movie *Meera*.

NMK: I believe at one time you had a problem with Raj Kapoor and this was in some way connected to your brother.

LM: We did have a falling out in the late '70s when *Satyam Shivam Sundaram* was being made. Raj Kapoor came to Hridaynath and offered him the film. I had to leave for the US and Mukesh Bhaiya was with me. When we were in the

US, Mukesh Bhaiya said: 'Hridaynath won't be composing the music for *Satyam Shivam Sundaram*. Laxmikant-Pyarelal are going to do the film.' I didn't pay much attention to his comment.

I returned to Bombay when the tour was over and discovered Raj Kapoor had indeed changed his mind and gone to Laxmikant-Pyarelal — despite first offering the film to Hridaynath. It was possible Laxmikant managed to persuade Raj Kapoor to use them since their music in *Bobby* had been so successful. Hridaynath was very irritated because he knew he hadn't asked Raj Sahib for the film — it was the other way round. On top of that, articles started appearing in the press about the whole incident. I got very angry and argued with Raj Kapoor and asked him: 'Why did you come to Hridaynath at all? I won't sing for the film.'

Pandit Narendra Sharma was writing the lyrics for *Satyam Shivam Sundaram* and said there was absolutely no question of Lata not singing the songs. Laxmikant then said they would not compose the film's music if I didn't sing. And so Hridaynath ended up persuading me not to drop the film for his sake. He insisted I sing.

When I went for the recording of the title song of *Satyam Shivam Sundaram*, I was still feeling quite angry. I sat down, wrote down the lyrics Sharmaji gave me and then Laxmikant-Pyarelal arrived and taught me the song. I took off my *chappal*s, as I usually do, and stood at the mic. Raj Kapoor said: 'Let's go for a take.' I sang the song once and the take was okayed. I put my *chappal*s back on and left.

NMK: How were your relations with Raj Kapoor after that?

LM: I had a professional relationship with Raj Kapoor and we carried on working together. On a personal level I was much closer to other directors like Mehboob Khan, Kamal Amrohi and Manmohan Desai. Yash Chopra has always been like family to me and I feel very close to him. Manmohan Desai loved my songs and his brother, the producer, Subhash Desai, was also very fond of me.

NMK: When did you first meet Mehboob Khan?

LM: I was rehearsing the duet 'Darna mohabbat kar le' for *Andaaz*, and Mehboob Sahib heard me. He came into the room and said: 'Who is this new Noorjehan? What is your name?' I told him my name. But he always used to call me 'Latabai.'

I remember when we came to record Majrooh Sahib's 'Uthaye ja unke situm,' there was a discussion about whether we should repeat certain *antara*s. Mehboob Sahib wanted the third and fourth verses to have repetitions. But Naushad Sahib said: 'Let's not record it.' We requested him by saying: 'Naushad Sahib, let's record the song. Everyone is here, including the musicians.' So we finally recorded the song in the way Mehboob Sahib had wanted it to appear in the film. The HMV disc version, however, is shorter and is as follows:

Kabhi woh nazar jo samaai thi dil mein
Samaai thi dil mein
Usi ek nazar ka sahaara liye jaa
Uthaye ja unke situm
Aur jiye ja yunhi muskuraaye ja
Ansoo piye ja, uthaye ja unke situm…

Sataaye zamaana ho situm dhaaye duniya
Situm dhaaye duniya
Magar tu kisi ki tamanna liye ja
Uthaye jaa unke situm…

She is the eldest of four sisters followed by Meena (far left), Asha and Usha.
Brother Hridaynath is the youngest of the family. Peddar Road, Bombay. 1960s.

His look of love once filled my heart
Filled my heart
That look is my only solace now
I endure his cruelty
I try to live. I try to smile
I try to dry my tears. I endure his cruelty…

The world torments me. The world is so heartless
The world is so heartless
Yet, I still long only for you
I endure his cruelty…

The third and fourth verses in the film have the repeat lines:

Kabhi woh nazar jo samaai thi dil mein
Samaai thi dil mein
Kabhi woh nazar jo samaai thi dil mein
Samaai thi dil mein
Usi ek nazar ka sahaara liye jaa
Usi ek nazar ka sahaara liye jaa
Uthaye jaa unke situm

Sataaye zamaana o situm dhaaye duniya
Situm dhaaye duniya
Sataaye zamaana o situm dhaaye duniya
Situm dhaaye duniya
Magar tu kisi ki tamanna liye ja
Uthaye jaa unke situm

NMK: Mehboob Sahib is right to have asked for the verses to be repeated because it allowed him to build and intensify the emotions of the characters as he cuts between Nargisji and Raj Kapoor and then Nargisji and Dilip Kumar.

I hear 'Rasik balama' was Mehboob Sahib's favourite song.

LM: Yes, it was. In 1958, Mehboob Sahib went to America for the Oscar ceremony when *Mother India* was nominated, and two days following the awards night, he had a massive heart attack. He was seriously ill. He could not travel and had to convalesce in America.

I was living in Walkeshwar in those days and his wife, Sardar Akhtarji, rang me from America to tell me the news. Mehboob Sahib took the phone from her and came on the line. He said: 'Latabai, I am very unwell. Can you sing me 'Rasik balama?'

I sang it for him over the telephone. A week later, he called me and asked me to sing the song again. And I did. Thankfully he recovered and returned to India a few months later.

NMK: Which *raag* is this song based on?

LM: It is a mix of two *raags*: Shuddh Kalyan and Bhopali.

NMK: Nargis mimed the song so beautifully in *Chori Chori*. You might record a song perfectly but what skills must an actress have to lip-sync it on the screen in the right way?

LM: If an actress knows something about singing, I believe she can mime a song correctly. Take Nutan, she mimed 'Manmohana bade jhoote' in *Seema* — it's a difficult song for any artist. It's a classical song but her lip movement is so correct, it seems as though she were actually singing. Nutan was a fine actress.

Meena Kumariji knew how to mime very well and so did Nargisji. You can see their neck veins protrude as they should when someone is singing. I liked the way they mimed songs.

The lip movements of many artists are rather slight and they don't give the impression they are singing at all.

Obviously I can't sing for any man — but when I watch Dilip Kumar sing 'Madhuban mein Radhika naache re' in *Kohinoor*, I can see the veins in his neck protuding. Dilip Kumar looks as though he is actually singing, not Rafi Sahib. If I had the chance, I would have happily sung for him! *[both laugh]*

Mehboob Khan was a close friend. At the premiere of Mother India, *Liberty Cinema, Bombay, 25th October, 1957.*

Left to right: Shakeel Badayuni, Naushad Ali and Majrooh Sultanpuri. These gifted men created exquisite songs for Indian cinema.

NMK: At some event, Shah Rukh Khan said his one regret was you could never sing for him! What about the generation after Meena Kumari?

LM: The names that come to mind now are Waheedaji, Nimmiji, Nanda, Sadhana, Sharmila Tagore, Sairaji, Mala Sinha and Hema Malini. They have mimed songs correctly. It gives me a great sense of satisfaction to see the variations and expressions I have tried to give the song work on the screen.

I liked Jaya Bachchan's performance in *Guddi* very much. I thought she mimed the song 'Baahon mein chale aao' in *Anamika* so well. There is a difficult song in *Lekin*, 'Suniyo ji araj hamari,' and Dimple's lip movement is flawless. Of today's generation, I like Kajol, and Rani, especially in Sanjay Leela Bhansali's *Black*. Another talented actress is Karishma Kapoor.

NMK: You have sung for three generations of the same family: Shobhana Samarth, her daughters, Nutan and Tanuja and then Tanuja's daugher, Kajol. Did you share a close personal relationship with any actress?

LM: I can't say I was close to many. I felt close to Nargisji and Meena Kumariji. We got on well and I liked the kind of people they were. They had a lovely, charming way of speaking. The way they dressed was lovely too — with their beautiful *ghagras* and sarees. I often visited Nargisji's house. She lived in a very gracious way. Meena Kumariji had a tragic life in many ways, but when you met her, you couldn't tell she was unhappy. Nargisji and Meena Kumariji were special people. I am also very fond of Nimmiji, Sulochana, Waheeda Rehman and Rekha.

NMK: Did any of the actresses insist you sing for them?

LM: Madhubala was the first who said I must sing all her songs — she even had it written into her contract. I always thought that Madhubala was influenced by Marilyn Monroe.

I later heard other actresses wanted me to sing for them. Male actors often insisted on the same playback artist. Raj Kapoor wanted Mukesh Bhaiya, Dilip Kumar chose Rafi Sahib and Dev Anand preferred Kishore Kumar. People came to identify a singing voice with a star.

To some extent Mukesh Bhaiya's voice matched Raj Kapoor's speaking voice. So it was a good fit. And Rafi Sahib's voice suited Dilip Kumar.

NMK: I heard a rumour that you are a wonderful mimic.

LM: *[laughs]* Even as a child I enjoyed imitating singers and actresses of the '30s and '40s. The first person I mimicked was my father. I was performing at a classical musical programme in Poona, and told him matter-of-factly: 'Today, I'll sit like you and sing like you.' I went onto the stage and did just that. Imitating his gestures too.

A friend of my father's said: 'Baap ser to beta sava ser!' [she's one step ahead of her father] Baba said nothing. He just laughed.

Everyone in the Mangeshkar family impersonates rather well. People often ask me: 'When you sing for Sairaji, how do you manage to sound like her?' I don't actually change my voice, but when I sing for Saira Banu or any other star, I think to myself: 'If I sing like this, it will look right for her.' So, I add some touch to reflect her personality.

NMK: Ultimately when the song is picturised, it acquires a life of its own and depends on so many factors. Which film directors for you have a good understanding of music and how the song can work on screen?

LM: Guru Dutt and Vijay Anand were the best. Although I did not sing many songs for Guru Dutt, I sang a few songs in his film *Jaal* and 'Badle badle mere sarkaar' in *Chaudhvin ka Chand* — the film was produced under his own banner. But I really liked the way he visualised songs. He gave importance and weight to every song line. He was careful about camera angles and how the actor should mime the song to make it work. He performed 'Aji dil par hua aisa jaadoo' in *Mr & Mrs 55* so well. He was so natural. I'll never forget it.

Guru Dutt was an intelligent and quiet man. During the recording sessions, he'd sometimes explain the way he intended to film the song but we communicated, by and large, through S.D. Burman.

I also liked Vijay Anand's approach. I believe Guru Dutt might have influenced him because Guru Dutt had worked with Dev Sahib. Vijay Anand filmed 'Kanton se kheench ke ye anchal' in *Guide* brilliantly. Another example of his skill is the *Tere Ghar ke Saamne* title song. Rafi Sahib sang the song for Dev Anand and I sang the *alaap* for Nutan. The scene shows the hero sitting at a bar and he starts singing. He thinks of the girl he loves and suddenly she appears to him in his whisky glass. Vijay Anand was highly imaginative. Chetan Anand was a good director too. And I liked Dev Sahib's acting very much.

NMK: Which other directors have created memorable songs on screen?

LM: Raj Kapoor. He understood music very well. He had a great sense of how a song should be picturised and explained to the music director exactly what he wanted. Raj Sahib would say: 'This is how I'll film it. This is where I'll cut. My camera will be in this position.' So we knew how the song would look in the film. His songs were wonderful.

Mehboob Sahib was very good too but had an older style of filming songs. *Andaaz* was different from his usual style. In *Andaaz* scenes lead up to a song. There's a party and Dilip Kumar is asked to sing. He sits at the piano and sings 'Tu kahe agar.' The child in the story has a birthday, and her mother, played by Nargisji, mimes the song 'Meri laadli, o meri laadli.' The same connection between song and story is made in 'Tod diya dil mera' and 'Uthaye jaa unke situm.'

Every song in *Andaaz* has a reason to be there. When songs are used in this way, the audience feels involved because they add to the understanding of the character while advancing the story. Naushad Sahib's contribution to the matching of scene and song in *Andaaz* was tremendous.

NMK: Bimal Roy's songs are also beautifully embedded in story-telling. Did you have many discussions with him?

LM: I didn't discuss songs directly with Bimalda. He talked in Bengali and I hardly spoke it at the time. He was a serious and quiet man and never talked much. He sat quietly in the recording studio and all he would say to me in Bengali was: 'Namaskar. How are you? Well?' Nothing more than that.

I liked his films. Whether his songs were good or bad wasn't important — the whole film was good. I consider him among our great directors.

NMK: What do you think of V. Shantaram?

LM: Shantaramji was an excellent director too. One of his special talents was his understanding of music. He couldn't sing but recognised a good tune. While the songs were rehearsed, he explained in great detail how he intended to film every song line. I liked his song picturisations in *Jhanak Jhanak Payal Baje*. The same goes for Yash Chopra. I like his films very much.

NMK: Gulzar Sahib is a lyricist, poet, writer and film director. What do you feel about his work as director.

LM: He is a different kind of director. I am fond of all his films — the serious ones and the comedies, especially *Angoor*. He is a stubborn sort of a person. I know this because I have worked closely with him on *Lekin*. He gets annoyed and insists on doing things his way, but what he delivers is of good quality.

Hrishikesh Mukherjee was a fine director too. He understood how to use songs well. He loved the sitar, and was very knowledgeable about classical music.

NMK: You started singing fewer songs from the late 1990s. But all the film directors of today, including Mani Ratnam, Sooraj Barjatya, Aditya Chopra, Karan Johar, Sanjay Leela Bhansali, Ashutosh Gowariker, Rakeysh Mehra – they all want you to sing in their films.

LM: And I have sung for them all. I find the work of these directors very good. I like Aditya Chopra's films. He explains the song situation very well. I don't see many films these days, but I liked Rajkumar Hirani's *Munnabhai MBBS* and *Lage Raho Munnabhai*.

Shah Rukh Khan can act in many different types of roles. In *Darr* and *Baazigar* he was a villain and then in *Dilwale Dulhania Le Jaayenge*, he redefined the idea of a romantic hero. An actor whom I like very much is Rishi Kapoor. He has always been excellent, a good dancer and is handsome too! I saw Aamir Khan's *Taare Zameen Par*. He is a good director and a very good actor. I regard him as a personal friend.

NMK: Do you remember which was the first Hollywood film you ever saw?

LM: I must have been around five or six years old when I saw Greta Garbo in *Mata Hari*. She played the famous war spy and I remember being very impressed by her. I have always loved Hollywood stars, including Peter Ustinov, Bette Davis, Gregory Peck and Charles Laughton.

NMK: That's an unusual mix. Which other Hollywood stars do you like?

LM: James Stewart and Cary Grant. I like Richard Burton too, especially in *Becket*. Peter O'Toole plays Henry II in the film and he is also wonderful in *Lawrence of Arabia*. The Bond films are very enjoyable too, especially the ones with Sean Connery and Roger Moore.

NMK: Do you have a favourite film?

LM: You will be shocked to hear the answer! *The King and I* with Yul Brynner and Deborah Kerr is my favourite.

NMK: You're right! I am a little surprised.

LM: *[laughs]* I would leave the recording studio once the work was done, and go to the New Empire Theatre to see a matinee or 6 pm show of *The King and I*. I used to go alone to see the film and have seen it fifteen or sixteen times! The doorman at the cinema would laugh when he'd see me rushing in. I loved Yul Brynner's character. It was a musical and Marnie Nixon sang for Deborah Kerr. Marnie Nixon had a small part in *The Sound of Music,* a film I like very much too. But I am not sure if Marnie Nixon was credited in *The King and I*. Another film I adore is *Singin' in the Rain.*

There are other excellent Hollywood films that I have loved, including *Death on the Nile,* which was based on an Agatha Christie book, and *Gaslight* with Ingrid Bergman and Charles Boyer. Excellent actors. Among the war films, *The Guns of Navarone* and *The Magnificent Seven* are marvellous.

I remember loving the old *Robin Hood* with Errol Flynn, and the 1948 version of *The Three Musketeers*. David Lean's *Dr Zhivago* and *A Passage to India* were so moving. And Alfred Hitchcock! I loved all his films.

NMK: Which Indian films have you been fond of?

LM: A film I have seen many times is Yash Chopra's *Trishul* because I really liked Amitabh Bachchan in the role. He is such a good actor. I liked his work in the recent *Baghbaan* too. His co-star in that film, Paresh Rawal, is good too. He can do any kind of role, serious and comic. I have always appreciated the acting of Uttam Kumar and Soumitra Chatterjee. Their Bengali films were wonderful. The work of Sivaji Ganesan and Chiranjeevi is also excellent.

Coming back to Hindi films, I am still very fond of *Madhumati* and *Dilwale Dulhania Le Jaayenge*. I liked *Sholay*, *Seeta aur Geeta* and Sohrab Modi's *Sikander* with Prithviraj Kapoor.

I was very young when I first saw *Kismet*, but I think I have seen it over fifty times! I used to have a VHS copy of *Kismet*, and would watch it over and over again. I like every aspect of the film: the music and songs and Ashok Kumar. It's a film I still enjoy.

I must have seen *Mughal-e-Azam* two or three times. But honestly speaking, I don't like sad films. I prefer comedies. I loved watching Mehmood and loved his *Padosan*. I prefer happy endings. *[smiles]*

NMK: When you mentioned seeing *The King and I* fifteen times, I was surprised to hear you went to the movies on your own. Did you attend premieres?

LM: I avoided them. In 1949, Raj Kapoor had a big premiere for *Barsaat* and invited my whole family and me. By that time, I had a big name and my fans had come to recognise my car. I had a light blue Chevrolet in those days. But I didn't feel like going to the premiere and asked my mother, sisters and some friends to go in my place. When my car pulled up at the Imperial cinema, Mai and my sisters came out of the car and heard the fans say: 'Ye to bekaar hain. Faaltu log aye hain!' [A waste of time. Some useless people have arrived.]

When Mai came home she told me in an irritated tone: 'We aren't going to any more premieres. We were called 'faaltu' [useless people] by your fans.' *[both laugh]*

NMK: Was the blue Chevrolet the first car you owned?

LM: The first car I bought was a grey Hillman. It was some time in 1948, and when I bought the car, I stopped travelling by train. I knew a car salesman called Mahajan and he offered to sell me the brand new Hillman at a good price. Mai had saved up some money, so we decided to buy it. It cost 8000 rupees which was a lot in those days — about 800,000 today. Remember I was being paid between 200 and 500 rupees per song. And it was only from 1964, starting with *Sangam,* that I was earning 2000 rupees for a song. So you can imagine how many songs I had to sing to pay for the Hillman!

I sold the Hillman for 7000 and bought a second-hand blue Chevrolet from someone in Indore. I gave the car to Mai to use. Some time later, I bought a Buick from actor Rehman — you know the character actor who starred in many films, including *Sahib Bibi aur Ghulam?* I also bought a second-hand Chrysler and then a second-hand Mercedes. But all the family loved the old Chevrolet.

There's a story behind the car I now use. As I mentioned to you, I considered Madan Mohan an elder brother and called him 'Madan Bhaiya.' And Yash Chopra considers me an elder sister and calls me 'Didi.' So when I sang the songs in *Veer Zaara*, I refused to accept any payment from him. When the film was released, Yashji gave me a Mercedes as a gift. This is the car I use now.

NMK: What about your staff? Have they worked for you for a long time?

LM: I had a driver called Jaisingh and he worked with me for years. He lived in our house in Kolhapur. He died in 1976. Many of our staff have stayed with us for years, including Mary who was the maid. She was from Malwan in Maharashtra and worked for me for twenty-seven years. She became part of the family. We had a cook called Sakharam but he has passed away too.

Mahesh Rathod has been my driver since 1996. I regard him as a *rakhi* brother, and respect him very much. I never scold the people who work for me. I always address them as 'aap' [formal 'you'] and show them respect. They do their work and don't need to be told what to do every minute. They must feel independent.

With Hridaynath and Pandit Narendra Sharma (right). A celebrated Hindi poet, Sharmaji was a close friend and guide. Photographed at a recording session for a non-film album composed by Hridaynath Mangeshkar with lyrics by Sharmaji.

Raj Kapoor (centre) seen here with his famous musical team. From left to right: Shailendra, Shankar, Jaikishan and Hasrat Jaipuri.

Below: Music director Shameer Tandon explains a song. Bottom: With Jatin of the celebrated Jatin-Lalit duo, whom she regards among her friends.

Below: (left to right) Lata Mangeshkar, A.R. Rahman, lyricist Prasoon Joshi and director Rakeysh Mehra during the recording of Rang De Basanti's songs. Bottom: (right) with director Madhur Bhandarkar; (middle of spread) With A.R. Rahman.

On Raj Kapoor's birthday, with leading stars (left to right) Dev Anand, Raj Kapoor and Dilip Kumar. Late 1950s.

Nargis introduced Lata Mangeshkar on the stage during the July 1979 concert at the London Palladium. For many years they shared a close friendship. Photo credit: Madan Arora.

At home in Prabhu Kunj, Peddar Road, Bombay, 1962. Photo credit: Dhiraj Chawda.

HMV gave Lata Mangeshkar the apt title: 'The Voice of a Nation.'

(Right of LM) S.N. Gourisaria, Nargis, Usha Mangeshkar and (left of LM) Sunil Dutt, musicians and friends at the London Palladium where a Lata Mangeshkar concert was held in 1979. The stage version of The King and I *starring Yul Brynner was playing there at the time. Photo credit: Madan Arora.*

The legendary Tamil star, Sivaji Ganesan, attending a Lata Mangeshkar show in Bangalore.

Madhuri Dixit's most popular screen song 'Didi tera dewar deewana' was sung by Lata Mangeshkar and is from one of the biggest blockusters of India, Hum Aapke Hain Koun...? *(1994).*

Sharing a moment with Mrs. Krishna Kapoor who is a close friend.

Portrait of Deenanath Mangeshkar by S.M. Pandit.

Portrait of Shudhhamati Mangeshkar.

During an interview, she was asked to read some letters she had received from her fans. The journalist discovered Lata Mangeshkar's fan mail filled countless files. Photograph taken in her Walkeshwar flat in the late '50s.

Studio portrait. Circa 1950s.

A rare photograph of the Mangeshkar family (and friends) at the occasion of 'Mai' Mangeshkar's 70th birthday. Peddar Road, Bombay. 1960s.

NMK: Can you drive?

LM: I am not a good driver. I get nervous. I find my mind wanders at the wheel and I can't concentrate for long.

Sometime in the 1960s, Jaisingh was driving me in the Buick from Poona to Bombay and on the way I met Umesh Deo, brother of actor Ramesh Deo. He asked me why I wasn't driving and said if I couldn't drive the Buick, I should try his car.

There wasn't much traffic on the road that day so I got into his car and we started off. There was a parked army truck facing us a little way ahead and when I saw it, I was certain I would hit it. I slowed down but sure enough I went straight into the truck and smashed the headlights. That was the end of my driving days. *[both laugh]*

NMK: What a shame! This may be utter nonsense but I read somewhere that you once said that eating chillies was good for the voice.

LM: It isn't quite like that. People say eating chillies or pickles, yoghurt, and sour food is bad for the throat. That's what some people say and believe too. But none of these things has ever affected my throat or harmed my voice in any way. I used to eat very spicy food with lots of chillies. I ate raw green chillies, not one or two, but twelve at a time. I could eat pickles too. But when I started suffering from colitis, I had to give up eating raw green chillies and spicy food. I usually drink honey in hot water when I am recording. What irritates my throat is cigarette smoke. And cigar smoke — just the thought of it! When I sing on stage, I request people in the audience not to smoke. During my concert at the Royal Albert Hall, I had a glass of honey in hot water beside me. Someone asked Dilip Kumar if I was drinking brandy! He laughed and explained what I was sipping.

NMK: There is a lovely photograph of you with a bicycle. Do you know how to cycle?

LM: I used to love cycling. Whenever I went to Indore to visit my aunt, and in Poona too, I would rent a cycle and ride around. But I never owned one.

NMK: Did you learn how to swim?

LM: Never. In fact, I have always been scared of water.

NMK: Have you any idea how many sarees you have?

LM: *[laughs]* I have never counted them!

NMK: Have you always worn sarees? Do you have any belonging to your mother?

LM: I always wear white sarees with different coloured borders. And Mai's sarees were of a variety of colours. I have kept some safely with me, but I prefer wearing white cotton. I buy my sarees from all over India — Bengal, Maharashtra and Kerala. I always choose the sarees I wear.

When I was about fifteen or sixteen, I started wearing sarees. Mai taught me how to tie one. The only trouble with cotton is that it gets crumpled easily. And by the end of the day, it doesn't look very good. The weather in Bombay is humid and hot, so that doesn't help. I have sometimes worn *salwar kameez* when travelling in the UK or the US. My father was conservative and didn't like us wearing frocks. Even when we were children, we rarely wore dresses. I wore *ghagra-choli*s in my childhood. There was a time in 1943 or '44 when I loved wearing *kurta-pyjama*s — the kind that men wear — a loose *pyjama* with a long sleeved *kurta.* I found them very comfortable.

NMK: I believe you are very fond of diamonds!

LM: *[smiles]* I love diamonds and emeralds too. In 1947 or '48, I had my first diamond ring made. It cost me 700 rupees. I designed it myself — it had small diamonds and in the centre of the ring, set in rubies, were the initials 'LM.' I wore it on my left hand on the third finger. I still have it. For many years, I used to wear an emerald ring that belonged to my father. But sadly it was stolen.

I never liked gold very much. But I do wear gold *payal*s. Pandit Narendra Sharma said no one in my family should wear silver. So we stopped wearing silver.

I once wore silver *payal*s, and Mai said: 'Chi! [disgusting] What are you wearing?' Mai never liked silver.

NMK: I read you went to school for only a day.

LM: I was at nursery first. The teacher used to write 'Shri Ganeshji' on the blackboard, and I used to copy it perfectly. I got 10 out of 10. While I was still at nursery, my cousin, Vasanti, was studying in the third standard at Murlidhar School. It was a Marathi medium school, just opposite our house in Sangli. And sometimes I tagged along with her. Whenever she had a music lesson, I used to listen attentively to the teacher singing.

One day, the teacher, pointing at me, asked my cousin: 'Who is she?' I jumped up saying: 'I am Master Deenanath's daughter!' She said: 'He is such a great singer. Can you sing?' I told her I could sing many *raag*s, and rattled off their names: Malkauns, Hindol, etc. She led me straight off to the staff room where all the teachers were sitting and asked me to sing. So, I sang a classical song based on Hindol. I was four or five.

Then the day came for me to join the same school. Asha was about ten months old. I took her in my arms and off I went. When I entered the class, I sat down with Asha in my lap. The teacher said firmly: 'Babies aren't allowed here.'
I was very angry and got up. I took Asha home and never went back. *[both laugh]*

NMK: You're so naturally bright, God only knows what would have happened if you had been formally educated!

LM: *[laughs]*

NMK: How did you learn to read and write?

LM: I must have been about three or four when I asked our servant, Vitthal, who was a teenager at the time, to teach me the Marathi alphabet and how to read and write the basics. I studied Marathi at home.

When we were in Kolhapur, Indira, my cousin sister from Indore taught me Hindi. She was from Madhya Pradesh and spoke Hindi very well and sometimes wrote stories in Hindi magazines. But there was little time to study because we were constantly travelling with Baba's theatre troupe.

When we finally moved to Bombay, Lekhraj Sharma who taught Master Vinayak's children, gave me further lessons in Hindi. Master Vinayak wanted me to learn the language.

Lata Mangeshkar loved riding a bicycle but never owned one. Photograph taken in the 1950s in Poona. Photo credit: Madhavrao Shinde.

A director at Prafulla Pictures, Ram Gabade, taught me English. I like reading in English and it is very necessary to know the language as it is so widely used in India.

I used to read Marathi and Hindi novels when travelling to work by train.

In the 1950s, a Brahmin priest called Hardikar taught me Sanskrit. I was very keen to learn Sanskrit because it improves your diction and I wanted to read the *Bhagvad Gita*. For short periods in my life, I had different teachers but I am mostly self-taught.

NMK: Was your father's family name 'Hardikar'?

LM: Some people say it was Abhisheki and others say it was Hardikar. But honestly I don't know the answer.

NMK: How many languages do you know?

LM: *[laughs]* Marathi, Hindi, Urdu, a little Punjabi, I can understand Sanskrit. Ihave also learned Bengali. Did you know the filmmaker Basu Bhattacharya? He was working as Bimal Roy's assistant and when I wanted to learn Bengali, Salilda sent him to me. I tried learning Tamil too. I can read and write a little but speaking Tamil is extremely difficult.

NMK: You are quite a linguist! What triggered your interest in languages?

LM: In 1946, I was working in a film called *Subhadra*. Shanta Apte, the famous Marathi actress who acted in classic films like *Kunku* which was called *Duniya Na Mane* in Hindi, was the star of *Subhadra*. We sang a song together and she told me she had recorded a song in Tamil. I was very young, maybe fifteen or sixteen, but when I heard her say that, I thought to myself, I must learn other languages too so I can sing in many languages.

NMK: I am sure the fact you have such an ear for music, and a mastery over words, must have helped you learning other languages. You have an unusual curiosity, a thirst for knowledge and determination to better yourself. How many languages do you now sing in?

LM: Thirty-six. *[both laugh]* I have sung in every Indian language, but also in Dutch, Russian, Fijian, Swahili and English. I was once performing at a charity show in Canada and the organisers knew Anne Murray, the famous Canadian singer, and told her I was performing in Canada. She sent me a disc of her song 'You needed me' and asked me to sing it on stage. So I did.

NMK: I wonder if you know how many songs you have sung?

LM: A gentleman from Indore, Mr. Chaurasia, recently wrote to me saying he had counted the number of songs I have sung and believed it is 28,000. Visitors come to his library and listen to his disc collection. HMV also told me they had worked out that I have sung 27,000 songs.

NMK: I am amazed you still have the use of your vocal chords after singing such an incredible number of songs! How extraordinary!

LM: *[laughs]*

NMK: You must have been close to many people in your life?

LM: I have always felt close to people with whom talking is easy and enlightening in some way. I am thinking of my relationship with Dilip Kumarji — I am close to Saira Banu as well but our relationship is of a more formal kind.

Bhalji Pendharkarji and his family have meant a lot to me. I regarded him as a father figure like Pandit Narendra Sharmaji. I shared a close relationship with Salilda, Naushad Sahib, Shankar-Jaikishan, Shrinivas Khale, Hemant Kumar, Mohammed Shafi, S.D. Burman, R.D. Burman, Sajjad Hussain Sahib, Vasant Desai,

She enjoys reading novels and poetry and is the proud owner of the entire Sherlock Holmes collection.

Jaidevji and Sudhir Phadke. Mehboob Sahib was dear to me, as were Sunil Dutt and Mehmood. In fact, Mehmood used to visit our home often. Not only have Majrooh Sahib, Chitragupt, Raj Kapoor and Sivaji Ganesan been close friends, but I am also very fond of their families.

Other friends in the film world include Khayyam Sahib, Jatin-Lalit, the young composer, Mayuresh Pai, Padma Sachdev, Surinder Singh, Ameen Sayani, Anil Mohile, Harish Bhimani, the singers P. Sushila, Suresh Wadkar and Sonu Nigam. Among the lyricists, I have great regard for Javed Akhtar Sahib, Gulzar Sahib and the Marathi poet Grace. The celebrated Marathi poetess, Professor Shanta Shelke, was not only a friend, but also part of our family.

Mr. and Mrs. Yash Chopra and I share a special bond and Yashji thinks of me as a sister. I always regarded Madan Mohan as my brother, so his son, Sanjeev Kohli, is no different than a son to me.

NMK: What about your friends outside of the film world?

LM: Nalini Mhatre was a close friend, as was Dr. R.P. Kapoor. Other dear friends are R.P. Goenka and Sushila Goenka, B.K. Birla, N.K.P. Salve, Pankaj Khimji, Subhash Bhoje, Mr. Shriram Gogate and Chetan Dhowan and their respective families. Old family friends include Balasaheb Thackeray and his family, Raj Singh Dungarpur, the Raj Thackeray family, L.K. Advani, Sharad Pawar and their families. I regard Icchubhai Parmar, S.N. Gourisaria, Mr. and Mrs. Raj Gopal Dhoot, Praful Shah and Shilpa Shah, Dr. J.T. and Mrs. Smita Shah, Nargis Godha, Dr. Sandesh Mayekar, Manoj Mehta, Dr. Akhegaukar, Mohan Wagh, Professor Ram Shewalkar, Vachaspati Shankar Abhyankar, Shankar Vaidya, Sajjan Deora, Rashesh Shah, Dr. Rajeev Sharma, Dr. D. Kelkar and Baba Sahib Purandarey and his son, Prasad, among my friends.

They have all been good friends to me and it is important for me to include them here. You might be interested to know that I also regard you as a friend.

NMK: It means a lot to me you're saying so. I feel a bit unworthy. What about your family? You are so close-knit.

LM: I am extremely close to everyone in my family. Among my nieces and nephews, I am particularly close to my niece Rachana Shah. I am very fond of her. I have always regarded Hridaynath not only as a brother, but as a son and a guru. He means the world to me.

NMK: Did some of your friendships sour and others improve with time?

LM: There was a time when Shammi Kapoor and I argued a lot. Every time we met at a recording, we would end up quarrelling. He was outspoken and said hurtful things. I would get very angry. But now we have become good friends. He is so unwell and on dialysis, but we still try and meet. His wife, Neelaji, is lovely. So this can happen too — at first you quarrel and then later in life, you become friends.

NMK: I have read some of the articles you wrote in *Filmfare* in the 1960s. Have you ever thought of writing an autobiography?

LM: I used to write a diary for years. I wrote some stories and songs in Hindi. Then one day I decided there was no point and I tore it all up and threw it away. I never wanted to write an autobiography because I believe you have to be totally honest when you write. And it would hurt too many people. What's the point in hurting people? My life and my experiences are so personal to me. Why write? It's all so personal. There's no need to tell the world.

NMK: Do you see yourself as a private person?

LM: I think I am. I don't give many interviews. I don't often talk to the press. The media often looks at the surface of things. What colours everything today is money, money and money.

NMK: That seems to be true. And with the mushrooming of so many television channels, the media is now like a monster that must be fed daily. And fortunately or unfortunately, Hindi cinema occupies a lot of airtime — sometimes to the detriment of all other art forms. Do you watch much TV?

LM: No, not very often. I used to watch a few serials and enjoyed the Mahabharat. I found *Mind Your Language* entertaining. But I have stopped watching serials now. Occasionally I watch an old film on television. And sometimes the news, but it's all so disturbing that I don't have the heart to watch.

Maybe there is a bit too much attention given to films and the film world on TV these days. I am not sure it's a good thing.

NMK: The person to whom you were particularly close was Pandit Narendra Sharmaji. When did you first meet him?

LM: In 1946. He wrote some songs for the films in which I was acting — this was during the days I was working with Master Vinayak. Whenever Sharmaji came to the studio, I sat by him and listened to him reciting poetry. He wrote in Hindi. So I met him very often. But then some years passed and we didn't meet. He was working as a producer at *Vividh Bharati* [the popular service of All India Radio] and someone mentioned he often talked about me. I started going to his house again. He lived in Khar. His wife, three daughters, son and daughter-in-law have always regarded me like a family member.

NMK: What did you both talk about?

LM: We spoke of many things: the Ramayan and the Mahabharat. I learned a lot from him. I called him Papa, and he called me his daughter. When I visited him, he used to say: 'What troubles my daughter today?' If I went to see him on a day I was unwell, suffering from colitis or terrible back pain or whatever — he would give me ayurvedic medicine. He reassured me and I would feel well again.

I often asked Panditji: 'What is life all about? How to cope?' We are sometimes overwhelmed by problems and get upset. Listening to him gave me such peace of mind. I ended up feeling I was worrying for no reason. The truth is one should not shy away from problems. One must face them. This is what I learned from Panditji.

I asked his advice about everything. If a family member was unwell, I asked him to consult his or her horoscope. Panditji was very knowledgeable about astrology. He didn't discuss my horoscope with me but advised me when a good period or a not so good period was ahead. What work might bring success and what work I should refuse.

NMK: Your belief in astrology must have come from your father and his interest in the subject. Did your father ever read your horoscope?

LM: He did and said: 'Lata will be unimaginably famous. But I won't be there to witness her success.' He also said I would look after the whole family and run the house, but would not marry.

NMK: How did that make you feel?

LM: I was too young at the time to understand what being unmarried would mean.

NMK: Do you regret not marrying or do you think — well, that's life?

LM: It *is* life. Marriage is predestined. You have no control on three things: birth, death and marriage. It's all in His hands. God decides. Perhaps if I had married, my life would have been completely different. Thanks to the blessings of my parents, gurus and above all, thanks to God, I am where I am today. I had the good fortune, since the late '40s, of becoming more and more well known. I have received so many awards, including the highest civilian honour in our country, the Bharat Ratna. I am deeply grateful for all this.

But ultimately none of it has affected me. I consider myself an ordinary person. The only thing I now wish is never to harm or hurt anyone. The older I get, I find living a peaceful and quiet life has greater appeal to me. I prefer to stay at home rather than go out.

NMK: If you had married, you might have led a very different life. I wonder if music would have so consumed you. Do you ever feel lonely?

LM: No, not really. I never feel lonely. Remember I have always lived with my family. I grew up in my family. When I was young, I had many responsibilities, but I was always made to feel like a protected child. It was Mai who was the eldest in the family and it was she who looked after us all. She was only thirty-six or thirty-seven when my father died. She was a very peaceful person, tolerant and patient.

When she passed away in 1995, I felt her loss deeply. It was then that I became the head of the family. I had to grow up.

NMK: Do you resemble your mother?

LM: I think I look like her. Perhaps I'm close to her in temperament. But definitely not in singing. Mai couldn't sing at all! *[laughs]*

NMK: I wonder whether your parents ever appear to you in your dreams?

LM: Sometimes they do. But they don't say anything. My father passed away in 1942, and I came to Bombay for the first time in 1943 to sing on stage. I was staying at the home of my paternal aunt and her husband. Another uncle was there too. Sometime in the afternoon I started rehearsing for the next day's performance when both my uncles scolded me harshly saying I didn't sing well, and what did I think I was doing by performing in public. I listened to them but said nothing.

I went inside my room and cried and cried. I fell asleep with tears in my eyes and dreamt my father was standing on the stage singing 'Shura mi vandile.' I woke up later at 5 that evening and told my aunt about the dream. She said: 'Your music programme will go well. Your father has blessed you.'

At 9 the next morning, I went to the Opera House where the music programme was held. I sang two songs. The audience was thrilled and clapped loudly. I was forced to sing an encore. The actress Lalitha Pawar was there too and she gave me 25 rupees in appreciation. Someone else gave me gold earrings and said they were so moved.

NMK: What kind of dreams do you have?

LM: Vivid dreams. I remember some but not all. Some dreams are abstract and unclear. I have never for instance dreamt of recording a song!

When I was about twenty or twenty-one, I used to have a recurring dream, in which I would see a temple made of black stone. I don't know which God was associated with the temple, but it was by the sea. It is early morning in the dream and I am alone. I enter the temple and open the door at the back of the temple. I see a few steps leading to the sea. I sit on the steps and the waves gently wash over my feet.

NMK: What a beautiful and amazing dream! It is so symbolic.

LM: When I told Mai about the dream and how it kept coming back again and again, she said: 'God has blessed you. One day you will be very famous.'

NMK: And the dream came true thanks to your talent and hard work. You are clearly a self-made person.

LM: I have always depended on myself. In that sense, I am a self-made person. I have learned how to fight. I have never been scared of anyone. I am quite fearless. But I never imagined I would get as much as I have. There aren't many people still alive whom I am close to, and can talk with— people who are older to me have passed away. I used to discuss things with Bhalji Pendharkar and then with Pandit Narendra Sharma. Now they are gone. Sometimes I talk to Sai Baba of Shirdi. I stand before his photograph and speak to him. I believe in Sai Baba.

For many years, I regarded Shri Krishna Sharma who was known as the Jammu Maharaj, as my guru. He was a famous man. I met Maharajji in 1974. He gave me a blue sapphire to wear round my neck. I wore it at my first international concert at the Royal Albert Hall in 1974. He did a lot for me. I was once in Hong Kong rehearsing for a concert and there were people smoking in the hall. The air conditioning was on full blast. I fell very ill with a terrible throat infection. A Chinese doctor came to see me and said my voice had been badly affected. In fact, I lost my voice and could hardly speak. I kept calling Maharajji all day long, but could not get through. When I finally got through to him on the telephone, I explained the situation. Maharajji said there was nothing to worry about and I should just keep sipping some honey mixed in warm water and a clove. Then I went onto the stage and thanks to his advice, I managed to sing.

Maharajji lived in Jammu but had an *ashram* both in Jammu and Delhi and so visited Delhi very often. He has a home in London where his son now lives. No matter where he would be, I used to call him every day. He cured all my ailments. When I had a problem of any sort, he would advise me on what I should do. I developed arthritis, and he helped me control it. I do not know how he did it, but the minute he saw me, he knew exactly what was wrong. When Maharajji passed away in 1992, I was very upset. And soon after that, my arthritis got worse. As long as he was there, I had his blessings.

NMK: How important is religion to you?

LM: I believe in God and everyone in the family does too. Whatever we have is thanks to His benevolence. No matter what you choose to call Him: Allah, Ishwar or God. He gives everything to us. I always bow before God and say: 'You have granted me everything.' I can never forget this. I pray in the morning and at night before I sleep.

I prefer silence nowadays to talking a lot. I'm not always in a mood to talk. I am at home most of the time. I listen to music and read. If I feel like talking to someone, I telephone a friend.

NMK: What music do you listen to? What do you read?

LM: I listen to classical music. Bade Ghulam Ali Khan, Amir Khan or Bhimsen Joshi. Sometimes I listen to *ghazal*s by Mehdi Hassan or Ghulam Ali. I enjoy reading Hindi and Marathi novels. And I love detective stories! I am the proud owner of the entire Sherlock Holmes collection. I also like Ghalib and his contemporaries, Zauq and Momin. Hindi and Marathi poetry is something I enjoy too.

NMK: You must hear your voice nearly everywhere you go. Does it still make an impression on you?

LM: I feel nothing now. When I first started singing, I would get excited hearing my songs on the radio. I listened to people talking about them, and used to find out how many of my records had sold. But as time passed, I lost interest. Now when I hear my songs, I think I could have sung them better. I didn't sing them well enough. I should have added something that isn't there. I am never quite satisfied with my singing.

NMK: It's funny how often artists feel this sense of dissatisfaction. It is believed that Orson Welles refused to see his films once they were made because he could spot all the flaws. But there's no undoing the past. Do you have any regrets?

LM: Since I was a child, I had always wanted to meet Saigal Sahib. When I was very young I would say: 'When I grow up, I'll marry Saigal.' Jokingly, my father would reply: 'By that time he will be an old man.' 'Never mind, I'll still marry him.' I do regret that I never managed to meet Saigal Sahib. Thanks to his brother, Mahendra Saigal, I met Saigal Sahib's wife, Asha Raniji, and his children. His son gave me a ring that belonged to Saigal Sahib.

Similarly when Dilip Kumar was working in films as a hero, I regret never seeing him at work — that's another unfulfilled desire. He can no longer be the hero of a film. But when I see his old films, I think to myself: 'If only I had watched him filming this scene. I wonder how he approached it.' I really like Dilip Kumar's films and have seen many of them more than once. He has acted in such a wide variety of roles and is exceptionally good. Ashok Kumar, Motilal and Balraj Sahni are actors whom I also like a lot. They brought such grace and dignity to the screen.

I have sung so many films songs and some songs had a classical base — but I really wanted to sing classical music and achieve some sort of name in the field. That never happened. I don't know how successful I would have been if I had tried. That's another desire that remains unfulfilled.

NMK: How has success impacted on your thinking? Do you think it is bad for creativity?

LM: No. You must not let success go to your head. I am very grateful to God that my success hasn't had a detrimental effect on me. My head could have turned; I could have thought no end of myself. But I consider myself to be nothing. I believe whatever has happened is His will. And the day He believes it should not be so, everything can turn to dust.

If I am gifted, it is by the grace of God. Who could have imagined I would be so famous? All right, I can sing but my singing wasn't some sort of miracle. My singing

Lata Mangeshkar considered Maharajji (left) her guru. She called him everyday for advice and guidance. Seen here with brother Hridaynath. 1970s.

is nothing extraordinary. Many have sung better than me, but perhaps they didn't get as much as I did. It is His kindness alone. So how could I lose my head?

NMK: Some people may think you have all the success in the world. What could you lack? Yet, it sounds like you are still searching for answers to bigger questions.

LM: I have seen a lot in life. My thinking has changed with age and time. I don't regret anything in the past, but for the future, I want to be sure I'll never do anything to harm anyone. In fact, I want to do things to help people. For example, I would like to help orphans. Together with my family, we opened the Deenanath Mangeshkar Hospital and Research Center in Poona on 1st November, 2001. The hospital was inaugurated by Atal Bihari Vajpayeeji, the then Prime Minister and the guests included L.K. Advaniji, Manohar Joshiji, Vilasrao Deshmukh [former Chief Minister of Maharashtra], and P.C. Alexander [former Governor of Maharashtra].

At the inauguration ceremony, Atal Bihari Vajpayeeji said he wished the hospital great success, but that if it was successful, it would mean a lot of people needed medical care and if they didn't, the hospital wouldn't do well. A witty comment!

We recently started a trust to provide free medical care for orphaned children. Behind the hospital we have set up a Cancer Research Centre.

I strongly believe people should not bear grudges against each other and live in harmony as brothers and sisters. Then our lives will be peaceful and happy.

NMK: Your mother once said of you: 'The more she suffers, the more her art excels.' What do you think she meant?

LM: A writer, painter, poet or singer — all artists are sensitive and they often suffer. One must be sensitive or else there is no life. Life would be very dry. Only insensitive people for instance are capable of murder.

NMK: What kind of things upset you?

LM: I can't bear to see anyone suffer or hurt. I keep asking myself why is it happening to them? I empathise with the suffering of others. If I have a problem or am hurt, I manage to put it behind me. But I really can't bear to see others suffer.

I can never see a dead body. The day Kishoreda died and I saw him lying there, my blood pressure shot up to 200. My doctor advised me not to put myself in situations that upset me so deeply. He told me never to look at someone who has died. I can't face it. I fall ill. I couldn't bear to see my father when he died. And though I sat by my mother's feet when she passed away, I couldn't look at her face. I don't cry easily. But I get deeply upset and disturbed. My blood pressure goes haywire. It's all too shocking for me.

NMK: To lose someone is shocking and so terribly final. I am sure you also regret the absence of many people like Pandit Narendra Sharma to whom you were so close.

LM: How can I explain it? He reassured me about so many things. Time and time again. Panditji was many things to me. He was like a father, a brother. He was a great poet too. Before I became a playback singer, I read his poetry. I have sung his songs on the radio. One of his poems is still well known:

Aaj ke bichade na jaane kab milenge?

When shall we meet again those parted from us?

There is a huge vacuum in my life now that he has passed away. I really do wonder when shall we meet again those parted from us. *[pause]*

There are some people who I still miss every day. Many people with whom I have worked have died, including many singers. When Bade Ghulam Ali Khan Sahib died, I felt as though music had died. Amir Khan Sahib has gone too.

A very learned Maharashtrian once said: 'When you walk on the path of life, consider every beast and man like a guru. You can learn something from everyone you meet.' I believe that too. As a bee gathers honey, so you learn how to gather things. There are lessons to be learned in every situation. I have learned a lot from the people in my life, and I miss them.

NMK: What does music mean to you?

LM: It is my life and God. My prayer is music — it is like a father and mother to me. And thanks to music I am who I am today. People recognise me everywhere because of music. But the greatest thing I have received — whether from king or pauper — is love.

People send me many letters asking: 'Can we meet you? We listen to your singing. We want to pay our respects.' The love I have received is a great thing. No one has ever said: 'When we hear you sing, we feel like hitting you.' *[laughs]* No one has said that.

If I were to live a thousand years, I could not repay the gratitude I feel. People have showered me with love and prayers — and thanks to them I am still here with you.

To receive love is the greatest thing. What more in life could you wish for?

Throughout her life, she has been deeply religious. She has a temple in her home and prays morning and night. She considers herself a devotee of Lord Krishna and Sai Baba of Shirdi.

In the 1960s. Photo credit: Dhiraj Chawda.

Quotes (in alphabetical order) on the following pages were recorded in 1991 for the documentary series Lata in Her Own Voice. *Comments by Javed Akhtar, Anil Mohile and the Mangeshkar family were written in 2009.*

Javed Akhtar

HMV celebrated 50 years of the talkies in 1983 at a grand event during which many singers, including Noorjehan performed on stage. I was asked to write an overview of the history of the Hindi film songs and Shabana Azmi delivered the commentary on the stage. When describing Lata Mangeshkar, I had written: 'If you take all the fragrance, all the moonlight, all the honey in the universe and put them together, you would still not create a voice like hers.' But today, I will not use poetic expression or superlatives for her. Because you cannot find a superlative that hasn't already been used for her artistry. So here I want to be dispassionate and surgical.

In any art form, whether it is poetry, singing or painting, there are certain factors: in-born talent, honed craft, passion and an X factor — a charisma which cannot be defined.

Lata Mangeshkar clearly has a gifted voice. It is unbelievable. It is pure and clear as the finest pearl or crystal. It is so perfect. Then comes craft. Every singer must sing in tune, so what is so special about Lataji? A teacher of classical music in Bhopal gave me the best definition I have heard about what distinguishes her 'sur.' This learned man explained that if you take a strand of hair or wire, even the thinnest of these will have a centre. Lataji sings at the centre of the thinnest wire called 'sur.'

As I am myself an artist of some sort, I have come to realise that mastery over craft is very dangerous for the artist. The more control you have over craft, the more dispassionate and mechanical you can become. It can turn you into a cold person. Your art is technique now and no longer passion. When we start off in our working lives, we usually have more passion than craft. But when we master technique, we lose passion. It is very rare for an artist to hold on to passion when it is equally matched by craft. Because these two things are in a way contradictory: craft is total control and awareness, while passion is total forgetfulness.

You need both qualities. Simultaneously.

Lata Mangeshkar has impeccable craft, a great natural gift, and has not lost that passion. Merging into a deep level of emotion, into the feeling of song words and into the mood of the melody — all these qualities belong to a person who has a tremendous understanding of poetry, a very sharp mind and unusual intelligence.

Imagine all nine planets in the solar system lined up in one row. This happens perhaps once in a billion years. Yet, this has happened in the world of Indian music and this happening is called Lata Mangeshkar.

With one of the leading personalities of Indian cinema, Javed Akhtar.

Naushad Ali

One day in 1942 or 1943, a young girl came before my eyes. Today the world calls her Lata Mangeshkar. She was wearing a white sari. And I asked her to sing and she sang me a song. A few days later, she recorded 'Haaye chhore ki jaat badi bewafa' with the famous playback singer of the era, G.M. Durrani. It was a duet I had composed for *Chandni Raat* and she sang it with great feeling. She then sang my songs in *Dulari* and *Andaaz*. The first song we recorded for *Andaaz* was 'Darna mohabbat kar le' which was recorded by Kaushik Sahib.

I remember the poor girl would come by train to the studio, drenched, holding her umbrella in her hands. I used to offer her tea. She was always very affectionate. If I felt unwell, she would come to my house to see me. Her decency and her affectionate nature are praiseworthy. She has such intelligence and perception and immediately understands how a song must be sung. Her singing range is across a full octave from C3 to C5 and she can reach as low as G in the alto range. She can sing half notes too, and through time, has increased the range of her voice and sings from one octave to one and a half octaves effortlessly. Have you heard 'Bekas pe karam ki jiye' from *Mughal-e-Azam*? In that *naat,* she reaches F natural and sings an even higher pitch.

Some singers sing to make money. For another kind of singer, singing is devotion and prayer. From the very beginning, Lata has had this devotion. She sits in front of a statue of Goddess Saraswati and practises every morning, whether or not she is recording a song on that day. Unless singers believe they are remembering God through music, their singing will never have an effect on the heart. Lata's respect and love for music is a form of worship. When she used to record a song, she'd leave her *chappal*s at the studio door, as one does when entering a temple. Her actions proved she has never regarded singing as a profession, but a form of religion.

Rafi Sahib and Lataji sang many duets together and music lovers, unfamiliar with their names, have never said when listening to their songs: 'Mohammed Rafi is a Muslim and Lata Mangeshkar is a Hindu.' This is because music is a creed in itself. I believe when God created the world, He gave it one image and man then created boundaries. The one thing that has never been bound in chains is music. It breaks all frontiers, carrying a message of love from one country to another. In sacred temples in Ayodhya, Mathura or Benaras, people can hear the *bhajan* 'Mann tarpat Hari darshan ko aaj' [I long for the sight of Lord Krishna] and at the shrine of Khwaja Gharib Nawaz or Deva Shareef, a voice echoed 'Bekas pe karam ki jiye, sarkar-e-madina' [Show grace to the weak, O Master of Madina]. Those holy men, those sufis, did not know a Brahmin girl called Lata Mangeshkar was singing that *naat.*

When Lata first came on the scene, music directors such as me, and others more learned and experienced, including Ghulam Haider, Anil Biswas, C. Ramchandra, Khemchand Prakash and

Naushad Ali believed they looked like brother and sister in this photograph.

Shyam Sundar, were composing music. These excellent composers guided Lata onto a fine path. A guide shows the way but the traveller must have strong feet to walk the path.

Some places can never be filled. Kundan Lal Saigal, Mohammed Rafi, Mukesh, Hemant Kumar have gone and their places are left empty. May God keep Lata Mangeshkar alive and well for a thousand years. But I will say that her place will always remain empty. She cannot be replaced.

Jaya Bachchan has always been a great admirer of Lata Mangeshkar.

Jaya Bachchan

I was a bit disappointed that Lataji did not sing the first song in my first movie. I don't know why but a newcomer always feels maybe Lata Mangeshkar will not agree to sing for me because you are probably not that good and the minute she sings for you, you feel she has accepted you as a good actress. Then you see yourself on the same level as established film artists who have been miming Lataji's songs for years. It is a sign that you have been accepted by the industry as one of them.

If you meet her, she comes across as a very private and intelligent person with a lot of dignity. I believe, if we have a real style icon in India, it is Lata Mangeshkar. Style isn't only about clothes but complete personality. She has not changed with trends and fashions because she does not need to. To me, she is personality personified.

Since the 1940s, Lata Mangeshkar has sung for many actresses but her own personality is very evident. Whenever you hear a song of hers, you know it is Lata Mangeshkar singing, no matter which actress has mimed the song on the screen, even Meena Kumari, who was considered a big personality. When Lata Mangeshkar sang for her you never said, 'Oh, Meena Kumari's song was so wonderful.' You said: 'Lataji sang that song for Meena Kumari so well.' And she did such a good job that it sounded as though Meena Kumari were singing it. When I played the role of a singer in *Abhimaan*, very consciously I based my character on Lataji. I felt very close to her when working in that film. Especially when miming the song 'Ab to hai tum se har khushi apni.'

There have been many films that have done well because the audience has liked the acting of particular performers only because Lataji has sung the songs they have mimed so beautifully on screen. She has most definitely played an enormous part in the overall performance of an actress. Many of the great stars of the past have become immortal thanks to Lataji because of what she adds to the emotional development of the character. If anyone else had sung for the older generation of actresses, something would have been missing from their performance.

Today when you talk of the new stars, people often speak about them in a derogatory fashion. Maybe it has something to do with the fact Lataji is not singing for them — because she doesn't sing many songs these days. So maybe there is something missing. Or maybe we just have not found a voice like hers.

She has a timeless and soothing voice. Doesn't it remind you of a waterfall?

Yash Chopra

It is said that some people follow music, but of Lataji, we say music follows her. She can sing in every Indian language and has even sung in Swahili and English. I made a film called *Chandni* which was very successful, and so I decided to make a Telugu version. When it came to dubbing the songs in Telugu, I spoke to Didi. She said: 'I have sung four songs in Hindi, I'll sing them in Telugu too.' We called a Telugu lyricist and Didi made sure her pronunciation and expression were right. While we were recording, I could see she had no problem at all. No one could imagine this girl does not speak Telugu.

There was a song in *Kabhi Kabhie* in which two heroines sing different verses of the same song. I explained this to Didi: 'I want you to sing for both girls. Can you vary the styles?' She made notes on her page of lyrics and when you hear the song, the variation in singing is clear.

Yash Chopra has tremendous affection for Lata Mangeshkar and calls her his 'sister.'

Many years ago, I made my first film, *Dhool ka Phool.* It had a very sad lullaby, 'Tu mere pyaar ka phool hai.' Didi heard the tune, wrote the words down and in the first take she sang it perfectly. She turned to me and said: 'If I sing it again, it will sound mechanical. I'm going.'

Didi brings feelings and emotions alive, whether happy or sad. She has a God-given gift and God's blessing. She regards her singing with complete dedication and takes it very seriously. She can sacrifice everything in the world but will never compromise on her standard of singing. If she feels her voice isn't sounding right for whatever reason — after all she is only human and sometimes her throat isn't perfect or she isn't feeling well — she just refuses to record. We believe that Lataji is a form of Goddess Saraswati. We are so fortunate to have lived in her time. She regards me as a brother and sings for my films. When we talk together about work, or discuss songs, I feel a strange thrill spending a few moments with her.

Manna Dey

My first encounter with Lataji was way back in 1950. I had heard her voice and knew she was a new force in the music world. Soon after that, we were to record a classical number together for Anil Biswas. It was a difficult song and in the film, the hero is a singer and is supposed to teach the heroine how to sing. I rehearsed the song for seven or eight days and was fairly ready. Then Lata was called to rehearse. In a single day, she learnt the song so well — I thought she was singing it better than me. So I tightened my belt and got prepared for the recording. The way she sang — it sounded as though I wasn't teaching her, but she was teaching me. The heroine was leading all the way!

Some time later, we formed the Playback Artists' Association, and my friend, the late Mukesh was the president. Lata and I were vice-presidents. We would meet many times to discuss things. How to go about improving our lot, how to deal with different situations and problems with producers, and finally we would end up sharing a hearty meal together. Sometimes we met at my house and sometimes at Lata's house. Lataji would look after everyone, and after the meeting ended, we were offered some delicious *tandoori* chicken. Mukesh, who was a very dear friend, enjoyed the occasional evening drink. And so when Lata asked him: 'Mukesh Bhaiya, is everything all right?' He replied: 'Everything is fine but since *that* is missing, the chicken tastes more like crow!' But we were at Lataji's place, and having alcohol was out. Most definitely. She never liked it and rightly so.

I would not say we playback singers created history or anything like that. Playback singing was introduced in the 1940s, and before that it was the time of the singing star. Even my uncle, K.C. Dey, sang his own songs. Saigal Sahib used to sing his own songs, so did Pankaj Mullick and Kanan Devi. When playback singing was introduced, different singing styles were heard. When Rajkumarji or Zohrabai sang, each had a distinct style. Then there was Geeta Roy and her singing was different again. When Lataji came on the scene, I felt her singing was definitely far better than anything I had heard before. Her voice is also very cultured. Among us male singers, Rafi Sahib, then Mukesh, Talat Sahib, Hemant Kumar — we all became quite popular. We all had a different style of singing. But when Lataji sang with me, I was aware I had to improve my own singing because she was a perfect sort of singer. I had to be very careful when singing with her. All the other singers must have felt the same way too.

I have always felt singing for her was like prayer or worship. When she entered the recording studio, she would take off her *chappal*s, which we never did, but she still does. Singing duets with Lataji is an experience in itself. First of all, no pitch is a problem for her. She can sing any pitch. Naturally a male singer has better pitch than most female singers, but that didn't apply to Lataji or Ashaji. Suppose we were singing for Shankar-Jaikishan, I could see she could effortlessly reach all the high notes. She had no physical mannerisms whatsoever when she sang. She was so calm and collected. It was a real lesson to me. I have always learnt from her. She was a singer who would never falter or hesitate. Once she had made up her mind and rehearsed, she never made mistakes. I did, she didn't. No one needed to tell her what to do when singing. But I was told: 'Sing very low, now the higher note, go back a little,' and all kinds of things. When recording she would suddenly sing a *harkat* in a way that was electrifying. I'd forget my own lines.

I remember we were once singing a duet for Salil Chowdhury — a very entertaining song 'Aiso re paapi bichua' for *Madhumati*. Lata was asked to give some sort of an expression at one point in the song. So I sang a line, and as I finished, she sang: 'Ooyi ooyi ooyi'... or something like that. I was taken aback and stopped. She is alive to all situations, and as far as her singing is concerned, ask her to express any situation and she can do it. I think she does justice to every song.

I have memories of singing some great duets with her. Every time we worked together, I knew the song could have been no better. Remember when Lata and I sang:

Aaja sanam madhur chandani mein hum
Tum milen to viraane mein bhi aa jaayegi bahaar
Jhoomne lagegaa aasman

Come, my beloved
Let us meet in the sweet moonlight
Spring will come to the wilderness
And the skies will dance for joy

Lovely.

Rehearsing the song 'Aiso re paapi bichua' for Bimal Roy's 1958 film, Madhumati, *with Salil Chowdhury (centre) and Manna Dey.*

Gulzar

There is a quality of 'expression,' which is unique to Lataji. I am sure there are other good voices, there must be — but not everyone possesses the kind of expressiveness she has when she sings. Take the *Jaal* song 'Chandani raatein pyaar ki baatein.' The way she sings the word 'chandani' — actually feels like the moonlight. It sounds authentic. This is a great gift for the medium of cinema. Sincerity, devotion and truthfulness can be heard in her voice. And these to me are great qualities. Also, you never hear effort or strain. Whether the song is at the highest or the lowest end of the scale, it sounds as though she were singing without effort — she never sounds out of breath. There are many singers in whose voices you hear strain or effort. It doesn't necessarily disqualify a singer, but this is a rare skill.

I know for certain every artist's personality is present in his or her work. Those who know the artist can recognise certain personality traits while others may not. What are the elements in her singing that allow us to glimpse into her personality? For one, there is no pretension — she is who she appears to be. There is no make-believe in her personality or in her voice. That is why we believe every word she sings. If she sings of a moonlit night, a moonlit night it is. Her smile is also apparent. You can 'see' the width of her smile in her singing too. There is another abstract element — and I am not needlessly flattering her — but she is a very generous person. She gives freely. She shares freely. And you can sense that generosity in her voice.

I will tell you a story. I directed a series on Ghalib and in an episode, Ghalib's fourth son dies. Lataji happened to see that episode and immediately telephoned me. Her voice was choked. She asked me: 'Why must every poet have to endure so much pain? Why did Ghalib have to suffer so much?' She was empathising with the suffering Ghalib, who died some 140 years ago, must have felt. Those who aren't moved by suffering do not suffer. Suffering is a sign of an artist's sensitivity. The more sensitive the artist, the more he or she suffers. I believe it is a part of creativity. Suffering is emotion. I don't believe anyone has loved without feeling sorrow. The beautiful thing is — you love and feel the pain too.

We have been fortunate to hear her voice and live in the same era as her. I feel very sad for those who have died without ever hearing the voice of Lata Mangeshkar.

With Gulzar and Chetan Anand (right).

Sajjad Hussain

I was composing music for a film called *1857*. The Hindustani title of the film was *Gaddar*. We were rehearsing in a production office on the fourth floor of a building, and Latabai's guru, Amanat Khan Devaswale, happened to give singing lessons on the third floor. We were friends and visited one another. One day he said: 'Sajjad Sahib, I have a disciple, a girl, so gifted by the grace of Allah. She is so intelligent and so incredibly musical, a kind of musical genius. No matter how difficult the piece, she sings it at once. Every night I think of another intricate exercise to teach her — sing this *sargam,* or *taan* or *murki* in a particular way — and she sings it. She sings everything effortlessly. Now I am so worried. Allah, what can I ask her to sing next?'

I was amazed to hear him say this because Amanat Ali Khan, a fine singer himself, never praised anyone. He had a very complex nature. He was a recognised master and had a big name, and for him to speak in this way was most out of character. So I thought to myself, one day I must ask his young disciple to sing for me.

In 1950, I was working on K. Asif's *Hulchul*. It had a fine cast with Dilip Kumar and Nargis. It was the first time I called Latabai for a rehearsal. I explained the song, 'Aaj mere naseeb ne' to her. She is very intelligent and thought about it carefully and then sang. I was pleased with the rehearsal and the song was recorded.

As it happened that particular song was deleted from the film. The producers finally gave it to another company. I didn't complete *Hulchul* because they hadn't paid me. Perhaps someone else finished the film. But I did compose three songs for the film: a *mujra*, and two other songs by Latabai, which included 'Aaj mere naseeb ne.' Sometime later, I heard 'Aayega aanewala' from *Mahal*.

I think it was Khemchand's song. That's when I thought-to myself: 'Amanat Khan Devaswale was absolutely right. This girl is bound to be a brilliant singer one day.'

The quality and purity of her voice, presentation, performance, *sureelapan*, the way she feels the words and tries to give a sense of what the words mean – these are her talents.

Thanks to Allah, I was very happy to have found such an elegant singer. And I decided that whenever I needed a singer, my first condition would be: 'I will only sign the contract if Latabai sings or else I won't.' Filmmakers are always in a tearing hurry, and if only I happened to have no other choice, did I use another singer — say if she was unwell and couldn't come to the recording. I always asked her to sing my songs, whether it was for a big or small film. I could see no singer better than her. If they had existed, they would be visible. Good singers cannot be hidden.

The most important thing in music is 'sur.' Music is nothing without tunefulness. If someone sings out of tune, then the musical value of a song is nil. Whether classical music, film music, a *ghazal* or a *bhajan* — she sings everything perfectly in tune.

Great Hindu and Muslim classical singers, classical musicians, and laymen say she sings without compare. Other playback singers and people who know how to appreciate good music, all say the same thing. And without doubt, she is without compare. No one can equal her intelligence. Nor can anyone equal her simplicity. She has such grasping power — and understands a song like no one else.

Anyone who sings without really understanding the words cannot feel them. How can they? That is why she decided to learn Urdu and made sure she pronounced and understood all the difficult words. She understands good poetry and just how intoxicating words can be. Once you know the word meanings, they touch the heart.

Everyone wants to listen to a good singing voice. That's why music-lovers have no choice but to admit that Latabai is without compare. That's how I understand it.

One of Sajjad Hussain's most memorable songs is 'Ai dilrubaa nazaaren mila' *from the film* Rustom Sohrab. *1963.*

Khayyam

The first time I met Lataji was in 1947. She was recording a song for *Majboor* for the great composer, Ghulam Haider, who gave Lataji her first break. I found her voice very sweet. When the recording was over, I asked Ghulam Haider Sahib: 'You have given a new singer a break, but what are her chances in the future?' He replied: 'If she is dedicated to her singing, her success will reach the sky.' And that's exactly what happened. Her song, 'Aayega aanewala' in *Mahal*, was played again and again in different scenes in the film — and throughout India the song spread like some sort of strange magic. It was the magic of her voice. Soon every actress wanted Lataji to sing in playback for her. Every music director and film director wanted her too.

The songs I composed and Lataji sang were big hits, and these included 'Bahaaron mera jeevan' in *Aakhri Khat*, directed by Chetan Anand, and 'Kabhi kabhi mere dil mein' in Yash Chopra's *Kabhi Kabhie*. I did not explain in great detail to her how I wanted her to sing the title song, but she sang it as it was composed. She kept the same tone, singing with much heart and soul. I have no hesitation in saying that *Kabhi Kabhie* was the first film of mine to enjoy tremendous success — it even went on to celebrate a diamond jubilee. Sahir Ludhianvi wrote the beautiful lyrics and these no doubt inspired her. Children, young people and the old still sing that song.

Lataji never expresses an opinion. She never says: 'You composed a good tune.' Yet her face opens with a lovely, soft smile. Her eyes tell you the song is very good. That's how you know she likes it. You may remember 'Ae dil-e-nadaan' from *Razia Sultan,* directed by Kamal Amrohi. Jaan Nisar Akhtar wrote the lyrics and Lataji liked them very much. She rehearsed the song a few times and recorded it, using the dummy track that was recorded in my voice as guide. She asked me how the song should be sung. Then she sang it in every range, high and low. The particularity of 'Ae dil-e-nadaan' is that it embodies breaks in continuity. Her voice stops, and after a

With Kamal Amrohi during the recording of the songs for Shankar Hussain *(1977), a film directed by Kamal Amrohi. Photo courtesy: Tajdar Amrohi.*

gap of five seconds, the singing starts again. She sang the song with such ease and rendered it exactly the way I had wanted.

Lataji's greatest merit is that she understands the needs of every music director. She understands what he wants and what the filmic situation demands. She moulds her voice according to the character on the screen and adapts her tone accordingly. If the song is an emotional one, and if it seems right, her voice will tremble a little with emotion. She has a fine personality. Sometimes we have had our differences. But when we meet again, she has completely forgotten what those grievances were about. She behaves in exactly the same way as before. She never bears a grudge.

She pays no importance to differences in caste, creed or class. Such purity in a voice can only come from a pure spirit — pure in every respect — because music is undoubtedly a gift from God.

I believe God has given India a great gift in Lataji, and we are very fortunate to have worked with her, to have sat together and talked.

Khayyam during the filming of the filming of the Channel 4 TV, UK, documentary series Lata in Her Own Voice, *1991. Photo credit: Peter Chappell.*

Recording the duet 'Lage nahin chhute' with Dilip Kumar for the 1957 Musafir *directed by Hrishikesh Mukherjee. This was the only film in which this great actor sang on and off screen.*

Dilip Kumar

Asking what effect Lata has is like asking what effect magic has. I have sat by her many times while she has recorded a song and asked myself, 'What is the effect her singing is having on me?' Her voice felt like a sensation running through the body, a mild stimulating electric current touching mind and heart — its quality is crystalline and immersed in melody. Although her voice is thin, it has a superior quality. She does not neglect it as time goes by and keeps developing it. Her discipline in work and practice has not been affected by her success. She continues to be untouched by fame. It might seem as though she were influenced by it, but this is just an outward impression — perhaps to avoid intrusion. The artist in her has remained intact. She is a very self-contained person. She may give the impression of being a complex person, but she isn't. She chooses to preserve herself. She does not want other things to come too close. This solitude is an essential characteristic of all artists.

There are other good singers, but no one has equalled her refinement. It is very difficult for anyone to compete with Lata Mangeshkar because there is so much of her in everyone who cares for music. Her voice creates a tremor in people. I think when you hear something very beautiful, it has that kind of impact. Today's singers can never reach the heights Lata has, because their output is often filled with noise. Today's music is orchestrated noise and so no one can hope to equal her.

Many people tell me: 'You know in such-and-such film, you did something really wonderful in that scene. I can never forget it.' What is it? What is that special thing that has entered the psyche of the audience? I myself have forgotten what that was. I am sure Lata does not remember either what she has brought to her songs, but for other people, all the variations and inflections have moved them deeply.

Lata Mangeshkar's songs are a part of our lives and memory. That voice, the notes she sings, that atmosphere, that suffering, that happiness, that pain of separation. This artist's beautiful voice is imprinted on all hearts. Your heart bears her imprint and my heart bears her imprint. And so there are an infinite number of hearts that carry the mark of Lata.

Talat Mahmood

I first met Lataji around 1950. I happened to arrive in Bombay from Calcutta. And I was already fairly well known and had heard her name too. I liked her singing. In 1950, there was talk of us singing a duet 'Shikwa tera main gaoon' in a film called *Anmol Ratan*. As far as I can remember, I met her for the first time during the song rehearsal. That song remains one of my favourites — it has wonderful singing. Truly, she adds so much feeling. She knows Urdu very well and is a superb performer. In India, there is no other singer as good as her.

Another memorable song is 'Seene mein sulagte hain armaan' from the 1951 film *Tarana*. When I sang the duet, I was very new in the field and the film's composer, Anil Biswas, was a famous man. He did not know whether I could sing well, and with great difficulty managed to persuade the producer to give me a chance. For a new singer that's the usual problem: convincing the producer. The first song I recorded for *Tarana* was 'Jali jo shaakh-e-chaman.' On that same day, we also planned to record 'Seene mein sulagte hain armaan.' I liked the song very much because it had excellent lyrics by Prem Dhawan. Anil Biswas's tune was wonderful and the duet became extremely popular. And whenever I give concerts, I sing it as a solo. It's a very expressive song.

Lataji's voice worked well with mine. We both knew each other so well. We had rehearsed a lot together and knew each other's temperament. So when we recorded a duet, it sounded as though it were composed for us. Adding your own expression to a song gives the song feeling. In this respect, Lataji is a fine artist — she helps a lot. She puts so much expression in her singing, and that helps me too.

When Lataji attends a public event, people are astounded to see how simple and modest she is. When they hear her beautiful voice, they imagine she is a glamorous woman and when they see her, they are struck by her humility. How can it be? I too was taken aback when I met her for the first time. I imagined her to be an extroverted, showy lady. But the most beautiful thing about her is her simplicity and sweetness. Through that simplicity she makes her songs more beautiful.

She has not changed at all since we first met in 1950 while recording 'Shikwa tera main gaoon,' till the last song we sang together in the 1964 film *Jahanara* which was 'Ae sanam aaj ye kasam khaayen.' I haven't seen any change in her. Whenever we meet, Lataji greets me with great respect and speaks very warmly to me. I have said enough. Now I will hum a little, if it can help. I usually never sing without an orchestra backing me, but I'll sing a verse:

Seene mein sulagte hain armaan
Ankhon mein udaasi chhaayi hai
Ye aaj teri duniya se humen

Mansoor Ali Khan Pataudi, the youngest captain of the Indian cricket team, at twenty-one (left), visiting the recording studio, Famous in Tardeo where Madan Mohan, Lata Mangeshkar and Talat Mahmood (extreme right) were recording songs for Duniya Na Mane *(1959).*

Taqdeer kahan le aayi hai
Seene mein sulagte hain armaan

Desires burn in my heart
Sorrow fills my eyes
Away from you, where has fate led me?
Desires burn in my heart

Anil Mohile

It is a matter of great pride for me to be associated with Lata Mangeshkar who is known as the Melody Queen of India. Since 1972, I have worked as her orchestra coordinator for almost every concert held in India, as well as abroad. The most memorable were three consecutive concerts held on 11, 12 and 14 March, 1974 at the Royal Albert Hall, London, for the Pandit Jawaharlal Nehru Memorial Fund. The concerts have created history as Lataji was the first Indian singer to perform at the prestigious Royal Albert Hall.

In 1979, during our London tour, Lataji and her brother, Pandit Hridaynath Mangeshkar, thought of a unique concept of combining the British Wren Orchestra, consisting of 56 musicians led by Ed Welch, with an Indian orchestra. Shri Amar Haldipur was my co-conductor and the resulting concert was a huge success — so much so that on public demand we had the honour of performing a second concert of the same magnitude a fortnight later. She is undoubtedly India's cultural ambassador and, we, over a billion Indians, are proud that she is a citizen of India. Personally she has been like a godmother to me.

With Anil Mohile at Shashank Lalchand's recording studio. Bombay, 1991. Photo credit: Peter Chappell.

As I mentioned, I had the honour of accompanying Lataji on her tours. We have travelled all around the world, including the UK, the US, the Middle East, France, Scotland, Canada, Australia, New Zealand, West Indies, Guyana, Fiji Islands, South Africa, Swaziland, Thailand, Russia and Kenya. When we are on tour, we musicians are treated like family members while she is the head of the family. A sweet and unforgettable incident took place during a concert in Scotland. It happened to be my birthday (July 8th) and after she sang five songs, she announced, 'Today is my orchestra conductor Anil Mohile's birthday, so let us first wish him a bright future on this occasion.' This was so unexpected and I was thrilled by her kind gesture.

Lataji is a perfectionist. Two months before a concert, she will insist on having a number of rehearsals with her orchestra. She always encourages the musicians. During a concert, if a musician plays a wrong note — human errors can't always be avoided — she just looks at him with a hint of a smile, which says, 'Ok. It can happen. Carry on.'

God has blessed Lataji with a divine voice. Her voice has the greatest purity of pitch. I would say Lataji's voice range in base, middle and uppermost — all three octaves — is superb. She has sung *ghazals, bhajan*s, solos, duets and songs based on classical and semi-classical music. Her magical voice has given these songs an enduring impact.

Lataji is a devotee of Lord Krishna. For her, singing is prayer. On her song scores, she always writes the words 'Shri Krishna' at the top of the page. She values Indian traditions and culture. She is very generous. She has often performed at concerts held for the Indian Army, and at charity events organised for hospitals and people affected by natural disasters.

To me she is 'the Lata,' unique like 'the sun.' May God bless her with a long, healthy and peaceful life. May her haunting, immortal melodies continue to fill the hearts of billions of her fans spread all over the world for years to come.

Waheeda Rehman

One of Lataji's special talents is singing in a way that matches the personality of a particular actress. She herself has always said that she makes sure to ask who will mime the song on the screen, and sings in the actress's style. If I hear a song, before actually seeing the film, I know she has sung it for Meena Kumari, or Madhubala or Nutan.

A favourite song of mine is 'Aaj phir jeene ki tamanna hai.' We were filming *Guide* in Udaipur. Dev Anand went to Bombay to record the song and returned very worried. He expressed his concern to Vijay Anand and me: 'I am dissatisfied with this song. I don't like it at all. Who knows what came over Burman Dada this time. He usually composes such lovely songs.' We persuaded him by saying: 'Let's at least hear it. How can Dada ever compose a dreadful song?' When we heard the song, we all liked it and asked Dev: 'What's wrong with you? It's a beautiful song. It will fit the story, the music is good, and the singing too.' But Dev was adamant: 'I really don't like it at all.' So Goldie [Vijay Anand] explained: 'We've been waiting here for a month. Let's film the song, return to Bombay and view it. If you still don't like it, we'll come back to Udaipur and shoot another song in its place.' So Dev agreed and we shot for about five days. When we returned to the hotel at the end of the day, the unit members could be heard humming 'Aaj phir jeene ki tamanna hai.'

On the fifth and final day of the shoot, Dev admitted: 'Sorry, I have made a mistake. It's a lovely song. We don't need to replace it.'

Much of the credit should go to Lataji, not only for this song, but for many compositions by Burmanda. She understood the filmic situation perfectly, what the character might be feeling at that moment in the story and created the right mood through her singing. Before the song starts, there is a scene in which Dev Anand tells Rosie, the character I play: 'Yesterday you were like a middle-aged woman, tired of life. Today you're like a sixteen-year-old girl, free and elated. Flying like a bird.' Then the song begins. There's so much feeling in it. When I first heard it, and if I hear it now, after so many years, I still feel like jumping for joy, as I did in the film and think: 'Today I feel like living again, today I feel like dying.'

When the singer gives expression to the song, it becomes so much easier for us to mime it in the right way.

The miracle about Lataji is that she never thinks: 'I'm a great singer. I am Lata Mangeshkar. So, I can sing a song in any old way.' She never thinks like that. And nor should any singer. She has sung for the generation of actresses before me, and still sings today. Words can't adequately describe Lataji's talents. She is indeed a great artist.

Facing page: Lata Mangeshkar regards the fine actress Waheeda Rehman as a dear friend.

Lata Mangeshkar had the highest regard for the Urdu poet and lyricist, Majrooh Sultanpuri.

Majrooh Sultanpuri

We're talking about 1947. Noorjehan was the leading singer and there was no one to equal her at that time. And second to her was Khurshid. Mehboob Khan was making *Andaaz* in which Raj Kapoor, Dilip Kumar and Nargis were acting and one of my duets in the film — 'Darna mohabbat kar le' had to be recorded. Naushad said to me: 'There is a girl who sings just like Noorjehan. Perhaps better, but her voice is very thin.' Then he added: 'If she sings in tune, it hardly matters whether her voice has body or not.' So, at the rehearsal, I saw Latabai for the first time. She was a thin, rather simple girl. She came, sang and left. The duet 'Darna mohabbat kar le' that she sang with Shamshad Begum was a sensation — people went crazy. Mehboob Sahib called Latabai, patted her on the back and gave her his blessings. We recognised a new singer was born.

I once had a high temperature and a song recording had been scheduled for the following day. So I called Latabai: 'I know we are supposed to record tomorrow, but I have temperature and can't write. Tomorrow's session will go to waste. And the producer is in a hurry.' She instantly said: 'When would you prefer?' I asked: 'How long can we delay the recording?' 'Not later than four or five days.' That was the first time we talked. I realised at that moment how much respect she had for me. And I respect her a lot too — perhaps she isn't aware of it.

There was a time when Latabai used to act and sing in films, but she didn't particularly like the songs that she had to sing. She refuses to sing obscene or vulgar songs. When she records, she first asks which actress will mime the song on screen. What kind of character does the actress play? What is the mood of the song? Is it sad or romantic? She becomes the character, and the emotions the writer has expressed in words come alive. She recreates that mood, that feeling in her voice. These feelings come from her inner self. She has never tried to change the tune and sings it exactly as composed by the music director I have been told, though never witnessed it, that the other great singer, Noorjehan, used to apparently change the tune. You will notice the range in Lata Mangeshkar's singing is unlike Noorjehan's. Perhaps Noorjehan changed the tune to suit her style, singing only what pleased her. Lata's own likes and dislikes are put aside. She is more interested in portraying the character through her voice – that is why she is extremely versatile. That is why she creates a living art.

Sheikh Saadi, a medieval Persian poet, wrote a verse and the essence of it is: 'If your true self is that of a mendicant, wearing silk will make no difference. Wearing rags will not make you a dervish either.' These lines speak of the purity one describes as 'selflessness.' Selflessness is essential for all artists. She has this characteristic in her. If you visit her home, you'll see she does not live in luxury. I remember once she was very ill and I went to see her. She called me into her room. The room in which she lives is small — not large at all. When it was lunchtime, she said:

'Have lunch and go.' We met informally many times. Our relationship grew and deepened. She often came to our house and liked my wife's cooking. My wife taught her a few recipes and she learnt how to make these dishes in our kitchen. We felt at home with each other. That was how I got to know that Lata Mangeshkar is a very good, decent and high-thinking lady.

It wasn't as though good tunes were composed expressly for her, or good lyrics were written with Lata in mind. I believe, she was given pretty average songs, just as the others were. But the magic in her voice made her songs reach out to people. She made those songs immortal. I have not tried to praise her. This is what I feel. Though she has a right to all praise and my words aren't enough — I should have said more. Perhaps it's beyond me.

Our Didi…

Meena Khadikar

In 1947/48, Didi was composing music for a Marathi film called *Ram Ram Pavhana* and asked me to sing two songs. I told her I didn't sing but she insisted and said: 'I'm there. You'll be fine.' I sang a solo and a duet with music director, C. Ramchandra. Didi sang the songs to me and I learned the tunes. I am a coward by nature so I was very nervous in front of the mic. I asked Didi not to sit where I could see her and somehow recorded the songs.

In the 1950s, I composed music for a Marathi film which was called *Manasla Pankh Astat* and this time it was I who asked Didi to sing two of my compositions. But I was afraid to instruct her and asked my assistant to stand by her near the mic. Didi shouted and told the assistant to please ask the music composer to sing the tunes to her. So I somehow managed to do it! The songs were very successful and were much appreciated.

In 1963, I got married and left the film world. When my son, Yogesh, was seven and my daughter, Rachana, was five, I composed some non-film children songs in Marathi and Gujarati. It was the first time children's voices were used in songs meant for youngsters. Usually adults sang such songs.

When we were children, I remember my father used to think I had a good voice and could become a classical singer. But I was so young and preferred playing instead of learning music. Baba was a quiet man who was always very generous. He gave freely. He used to wake up everyday at 4 in the morning and an hour or so later, Didi would be asked to take the *tanpura*, sit by him and learn how to sing. We also sang in Baba's theatrical productions. We siblings learned how to focus and project our voices on the stage so that the spectators who sat right at the back could hear the songs clearly.

Didi was a strong-willed child and we spent most of our time playing. We also acted at home in the plays that she wrote. I usually played the vamp! Whenever we saw a film, we'd return home and enact scenes from it. I remember seeing the 1930s films, *Devdas* and *Sant Tukaram*. When we came home from watching *Sant Tukaram,* Didi piled up a stack of mattresses and sat on top of them, high above us. Our cousins and we young sisters lay on the floor while Didi sang a song from the film. The song describes how wheat grows — and so we slowly rose and eventually stood up and swayed like wheat stalks in a field.

Whenever we had *laddoo*s in the house for offering in prayer, Didi made us all go to sleep and pretending to be a ghost or a thief, she'd take all the *laddoo*s and eat them up. We were all scared of her and still are! One day, she was annoyed for some reason, and decided she was going to leave home. She took a small bundle of clothes, held it under her arm and started walking away from the house. Baba instructed us to do absolutely nothing. As she walked further and further away from the house, we could see that she kept looking back to see if anyone was coming after her. When she realised no one was following her, she turned around and returned home.

When Baba passed away, she looked after us like her own children. We are a close-knit family and are happy in each other's company. In fact, we can't live without each other. When you live through difficult times you always have your feet firmly on the ground. We learned the value of money and knew what it's like to be poor. In later years, Mai made sure we did not live in a filmi atmosphere. Didi never behaved like a star. And despite Didi's extraordinary success, she hasn't changed one bit. The young girl in her has remained perfectly intact.

With Meena who married Dattatraya Khadikar in 1963.

Asha Bhosle

As children, I think I was the closest to Didi. She used to pick me up in her arms and run all over town with me. We used to live in Sangli in those days. We were so attached to one another that she would even take me with her to school everyday, till finally her class teacher refused to let us both sit in the same class. When the teacher forbade us to be there together, we came home crying. And then Didi refused to go to school without me. Baba said we would have a private tutor and that was the end of her schooling.

I think our first duet was 'Ye barkhaa bahaar na ja soutaniya ke dwar' for the film *Mayur Pankh*. We recorded this song sometime in the 1950s. It was a challenge singing with her because I had always admired her as a singer, and besides, she was my eldest sister. Didi is an introvert. She is highly intelligent, but also quite fickle. Work is worship for her and she excels in music.

So many people have asked her about her singing, but if I were to ask her something, my question would be: At such an early age, how did you manage to infuse such emotion into your songs? Your voice and perfect pitch is a God-given gift, but to understand and utilise your talent perfectly at such an early age is something that bewilders me. As a child, did you ever realise that you were destined to be great? Were you aware that you were a child prodigy?

Usha Mangeshkar

The *Azaad* song 'Aplam chaplam' was the second film song that I sang. I was just terrified, but the film's music director, C. Ramchandra, insisted I sing. The only thing that appealed to me was the idea of singing the duet with Didi. I had heard her singing at several recording sessions and had observed how she would sing, how she would stand, how she would pronounce the lyrics — I knew a little Urdu and Hindi at that time. By watching her, I learned from her. The comforting thing was that I could tell Didi: 'This line is too high for me — you sing it. How do I sing this line? Tell me.' That was how 'Aplam chaplam' was recorded. The wonderful thing was two sisters performed the song on the screen.

When we sing a duet together, I pay attention to my singing, So we don't need many retakes. And Didi doesn't have to sing the song again and again. Didi becomes the song. It's something amazing to watch — she makes sure each word can be clearly understood. The music director never needs to tell her where she has gone wrong. She is fully aware at what point she makes a mistake and she herself calls for a cut. You can learn a lot by watching her. Perhaps other singers were afraid of her, but I have never been scared of singing with Didi. I enjoyed it.

We observe how she is at home. When she wakes up, she prays and before she sleeps, she prays. She is a very calm person, never fights with anyone and never loses her temper. *Bhajan*s suit her voice and personality — and love songs too, or 'slow songs,' as they are called.

I am very lucky to be the youngest sister in the family. I have been thoroughly spoiled: 'She's the youngest. Don't tease her. She's the youngest, buy her presents!' I always had my way and got whatever I wanted. It's true even now. Didi listens to whatever I say.

We never discuss films at home. All we ask her is: 'Whose song did you sing today? How was it? Good?

That's nice.' End of discussion. Then we talk about other things. Sometimes she tells us funny anecdotes and imitates people — how someone sings, how someone walks, how someone talks. She is a good impersonator and makes us all laugh.

We are scared of her because she is the eldest. But we all love her a lot too. She has a father's authority in the house. Mother once told us: 'She's your elder sister. But regard her as you would a father or mother.' And that's how we think of her and that is how she sees us — as though we were her children. She loves us like her own children and never lets us feel the lack of anything. When she goes out, she'll buy clothes for everyone. When she travels abroad, she makes sure we accompany her. She has taken Mai, our mother, all around the world and made it possible for us to visit every country we have wanted to see. We once told her we were keen to visit Disneyland and she took us there. She does nothing alone, so we all travel together.

When we have a problem, we go straight to her. But she never voices a complaint to us. Once she was very ill but never said a word. She just sat quietly. We insisted on knowing what was wrong. Then she said she was in great pain and we called the doctor.

There is an aura of peace as soon as she enters the house. But sometimes she can make us laugh a lot.

Photo credit: Asit Sen.

Hridaynath Mangeshkar

Few singers can sing in four octaves as Didi can. In Hindustani music the octaves are: *kharaj* [low], the middle, upper, and uppermost, a range of twenty-eight notes. Didi can sing the entire range of twenty-eight notes. The only other singer I know of who had this same gift was Bade Ghulam Ali Khan. His voice sounded good, even at high pitch. In the *Jis Desh Mein Ganga Behti Hai* song, 'Aa ab laut chalen,' Didi touches the seventh note in the fourth octave — the highest a human voice can reach. In the song, you hear her holding the note and not sounding shrill. She knows classical music well, having learned it from my father, and Ustaad Aman Ali Khan Bhendibazaarwale and then Amanat Khan Devaswale. In classical music, there is a light *taan* and a *ghamak taan*. If you do not equally master the *ghamak taan*, then the light *taan* alone doesn't sound very good. Because Didi has practised both kinds of *taans* in her childhood, she can sing them easily.

Another essential rule of classical music is hitting the note that falls on the beat and Didi learned this in her childhood and does it in all her songs. There is a line in a poem by Rabindranath Tagore, which says: 'There is rhythm even in the way one looks.' If you glance quickly at a wall, you will not see what covers it. But if you look at it with a certain rhythm then you will discover a picture, a clock and other things hanging on that wall. It is the same with music — one has to share the experience of each note alongside a rhythm. God has blessed Didi with this gift.

When, through music, we present the writings of poet-saints, including Kabir, Surdas, Meerabai, Gyaneshwar and Tukaram, and start researching their lives, written accounts can be found. But their true images do not exist – what is called a *praman* image. So when writing music based on their sacred work, the composer must imagine an image of the poet-saint. When I was composing an album of Meerabai's *bhajans*, I imagined how she would have looked. I painted a picture of her in my mind — tall, fair-skinned, slender — I also imagined the way Meerabai would speak. Once I had an idea of her, I thought of a voice to suit that image and found Didi's voice the most appropriate. I believe devotional songs suit Didi's voice very well. Her inner self is pure and simple and the lyrics in devotional songs are usually simple too. The simplicity of the lyrics and the simplicity of Didi's character — put these together and you find oneness of a spiritual kind.

In our religion, we say that *amrut sparsh* quickens the dead; this nectar is in Didi's voice. And when Didi sings, she makes many ordinary songs immortal. She lifts them out of the ordinary.

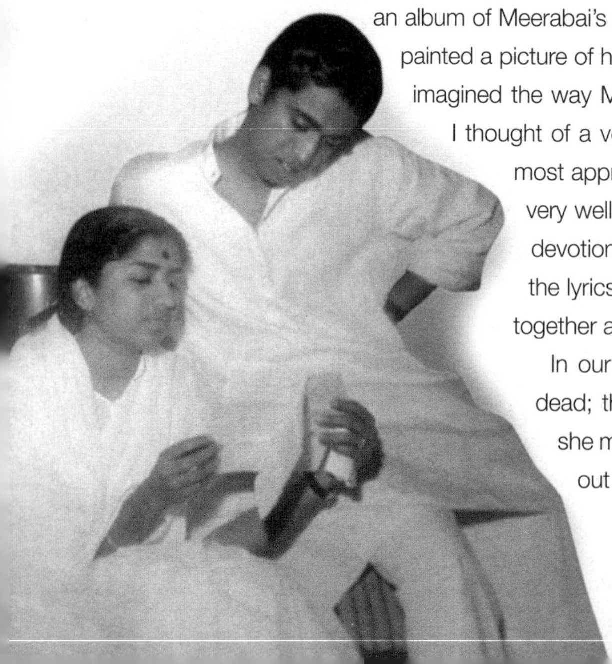

Bharati Mangeshkar

My father, Damuanna Malwankar, was a comedian and actor who worked in the Marathi cinema and theatre from the 1930s. He also worked in Deenanath Mangeshkar's theatre company and acted in many of the stage plays they produced. I believe it is God's blessings that he acted with Didi in the Marathi film *Gajabhau* and the Hindi film, *Badi Maa*, starring Noorjehanji. I grew up hearing Didi's songs and loving them. I acted in some Marathi and Hindi films and plays as well and all the Mangeshkar sisters have sung for me in playback. But I was always very sad that Didi had never sung any of the songs that I had mimed on screen.

The first time I saw Didi was sometime in 1965 or 1966. I was getting ready in the make-up room at Jaiprabha Studio in Kolhapur when the make-up man told me excitedly that Lata Mangeshkar had arrived and was going to walk past the window of the make-up room on her way to the Hanumanji's temple which was on the studio grounds. I was absolutely thrilled and stood on a chair so I could lean out of the window and see her. I waited patiently and then suddenly I heard the tinkling sound of her *payal* and I saw her. She had two long braids — I felt everything about her was musical; the way she walked and every step she took was musical. That memory is still etched on my mind.

In 1967, Didi asked my father to attend an S.D. Burman night, and that was the first time I heard Didi singing live. The entire film industry was there and it was a wonderful evening. After that, she invited us over on her birthday. This was the first of many visits to her Prabhu Kunj home.

I married Hridaynath Mangeshkar on 7th March, 1970. It was a love marriage and I became part of the Mangeshkar family. In all the years I have known Didi, I have seen no change in her. When my young children used to sleep with me at night, sometimes I slept through their crying, but not Didi. She would hear them from the next room and pick up the child who was upset and console it. It never mattered to her that she was sleepy or tired or that she had to wake up early the next day to go and record a song. I have given birth to three children: Adinath, Baijnath and Radha, but Didi has been their real mother. She is the pillar of our family. I am a devotee of her voice and always pray to God to keep her well and bless her. But I must admit I cannot adequately express my admiration for her as a person.

Hridaynath and Bharati Mangeshkar with their three children: Baijnath (left), Adinath and Radha.

Yogesh Khadikar *nephew*

To even comment on her musical talents is beyond me, I am just lucky to be born surrounded with her heavenly voice. On a par with her music is Didi's simplicity. While growing up, we were never made to feel we were living so close to a legend. She joked with us, played with us and even cooked for us; she was always there for us. When we went out to a movie, restaurant or to one of her concerts here or abroad, we saw the deep admiration in people's eyes — the love they showered on her. Then it dawned on me that I was standing next to a legend. I never realised her greatness until then. I think it was her personality, never to make us feel that she is a star. Sometimes people ask me: 'Ah, you're so close to her, tell us about her. Is she reserved and strict?' I must confess, I am often tempted to go along with that story and say: 'Yes, she is very strict.' But in reality, she is totally the opposite. She's fun loving, the most down-to-earth and sensitive person. A baby's cry or a stray dog's whimper makes her restless — it is this sensitivity, which translates into her songs and leaves an everlasting impression on the listener's heart.

Didi has never made us conscious of what she has been through — all the hard times. It is all behind her. It is as though nothing had happened. She is an ordinary family member like my mother. In fact, she is like a mother to me. I have always felt blessed to live under Didi's loving presence. In 2004, I got married to Mekhala, and we now have a three-year old daughter, Saanjali. I can feel Didi's affection so seamlessly extend to my family — Didi's love grows from one generation to the next.

She has such a sweet nature, and that sweetness is in her voice.

With Yogesh and Mekhala Khadikar and their daughter.

Rachana Shah *niece*

For six decades, this mystical voice has enthralled you, moved you to tears, touched your heart, stirred hidden emotions, led you to smile, breathed divinity into your homes, and made you proud of your country. Moments from the astonishing journey of this rare persona will, through this book, touch your lives in the way it has touched all those who are blessed and privileged to be a small part of it. The colossal persona, Didi, and the blessed one is me.

Simply put, Didi to me is a blend of a mother and a friend. Her being one of the greatest artistes is a known fact and I will not dwell on that. I would prefer instead to sketch the heart that beats behind this voice.

The world over, Lata Mangeshkar is the voice of India, the greatest singer and a living legend, etc. To me, Didi is one of the nicest and simplest people that I know. In fact, her deep sense of humanity is far greater than the artiste in her. I grew up with my Didi looking after me in every possible way. Children hold a very special place in her life and no child in her eyes can be even remotely bad. So, naturally we nieces and nephews were greatly mollycoddled and completely over-protected. But behind her indulgence, she never failed in lovingly instilling the right values in us. As for me, I think I grew up imbibing her values by watching her example. The way she cares for the staff in our household, the way she understands what you will say even before you have started to speak. Her love and loyalty towards the family and her close friends: her reaching out to people without them knowing it. She is always there for you like a guardian angel when you need her most.

When you meet Didi, the first thing that strikes you is her smile, a typical Libran smile that can melt the hardest heart, and the next thing you become aware of is her obsession with perfection. I have yet to meet anyone who is so meticulous and dedicated to everything she does.

I love my Didi, yet there is one thing about her that I just cannot understand. Why does Didi never speak up? It upsets me deeply to see her falsely blamed and so often maligned. False rumours were spread but she chose to remain silent. It disturbs me to see her hurt. But Didi is very philosophical by nature and feels that life finds a way of sorting things out. The essence of Didi lies in her self-respect and dignity and she will never compromise on that.

So many fond memories and moments fill my heart as I write and I know I could go on and on. In fact, I will stop now, go and spend time with Didi. I know that when I enter her room, the fragrance of incense will permeate the air. She will be relaxing on her bed and will greet me with that smile of hers — a smile that can light up a thousand homes.

What a lady she is. What a life. Unparalleled. This is what separates the ordinary from the extraordinary. Such is the spirit that legends are made of.

Adinath Mangeshkar *nephew*

My dear, dear Didi. She is a mother to me. Throughout my life she has been my guru, inspiration, motivation and singlemost source of happiness and peace.

The very thought that I was brought up by you makes me believe I have lived seven lifetimes — with joy and fulfillment. The love, concern, and care you have for us all shows in your eyes; we hear it in your voice, and see it in all your actions. Sometimes I feel I have seen divinity right here on earth.

Whether it was sharing a simple meal with you, or travelling the world with you, I have been the student, and you have been my teacher. Your simplicity, genuine humility, polite firmness, your thinking before acting — all these aspects of your personality have taught us so much and shaped us into the people we are today.

Performing with you in a concert or observing you rehearse — has allowed me to learn the mysteries of the arts. You have my deep admiration and respect for your thirst for perfection, while knowing how unimaginably hard you have worked to achieve this perfection.

You have made me love music and literature. Reality and spirituality. Life's battles are so easily fought if one follows your gentle guidance. You told me my grandfather had once advised — when in doubt, ask the soul enveloped within your soul to discover whether the actions you want to take are right or wrong, and if the answer is yes, then go ahead and never look back.

I see your smile. I see you laugh when you hear a joke, or tell us one. I see you face the adversities of life so effortlessly. How do you do that? Especially when we think of the trials you have faced. Losing a father when you were only thirteen years old, working day and night to provide for the family, looking after my ailing father, who was only four years old then. Despite the battles you have fought, you have given people unlimited joy through your songs. There aren't enough words to express what I really feel for you.

Every day I ask God to grant me two lives: one is for myself and the other is to give to you.

With Adinath Mangeshkar

Baijnath Mangeshkar *nephew*

Where do I begin? For 36 years, I have been raised under the aura of my magnificent aunt – the legendary Lata Mangeshkar — my Didi. And so to write a few words about her is a daunting task. Yet for the hopelessly shy, yours truly, there is an unexpressed joy in documenting forever the respect, admiration and love I have for her.

As a child of three and a half, obviously unaware of who she was in the world, my earliest memory is of a larger-than-life woman amongst the many wonderful women with whom I grew up. Yes, she was kind, loving, indulgent and yet strict like the others, but there was something conspicuously different — was it the wonderful fragrance of the French perfume she wore that would leave a trail long after she had gone to the studio? Was it the silhouette of a lady enveloped in smoke, as she religiously lit *dhoop* at the *mandir* every day? Was it her unusually long hair braided in two plaits? Was it the majestic and confident walk only equalled by the gait of royalty? Or was it the disarming tinkling of her *payal* announcing her entry and exit like the arrival and departure of a queen? I'm not quite sure, but all these images were very attractive and beguiling for an impressionable young mind.

With time and age, one realised the magnitude of her musical genius, but at home we were among the chosen few to witness and experience a wonderfully domesticated woman too. Her acts and stories of generosity, kindness and charity are well known. She has a remarkable, razor-sharp memory, especially with dates, and never forgets the birthdays of her friends and acquaintances. She also has a penchant for showering gifts on people. Being her nephew, needless to say, I have received innumerable presents and handwritten cards. Her short, charming hand-written inscriptions are deceptively simple yet profoundly wise and are always relevant to my age and to that moment in time.

She has probably forgotten a wonderful gift she gave me, which she actually made herself! I think it was in 1978. And inspired by the Disney series of 'hear-n-read books and audio cassette kits,' she recorded two short stories, just for me, including a personal introduction. Just imagine a recording of Lata Mangeshkar of a completely different and unique kind. Her ardent fans will be eating their hearts out! I have no words to express how special it is to me.

Beyond the fact that I am related to her, and from a different generation, her music is timeless for me. I am probably one of her most devoted fans — and the proud owner of a rare collection of her records. But I am afraid with the current reign of materialism, and increasing irreverence for the past, the next generation will probably regard her musical genius as mere myth — in the way Tansen's melodious voice is said to have had the deer of the forest, mesmerised and rushing to him. Her perfection in rendering extremely complex and difficult songs, which require tremendous vocal agility, mastery and soul, have mostly been recorded live with musicians — in one take —

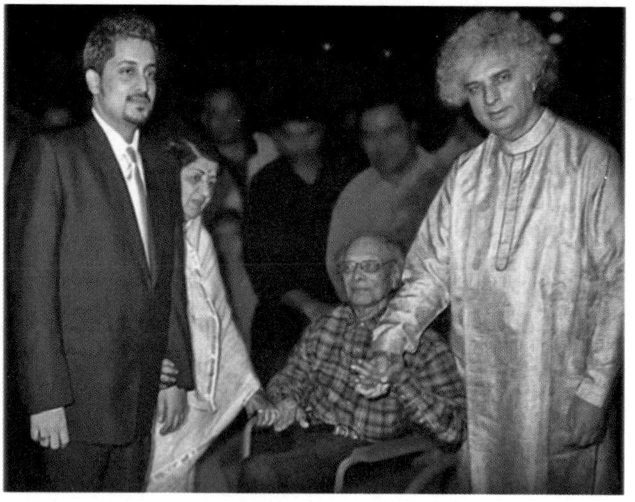

Left to right: Baijnath Mangeshkar, Lata Mangeshkar, Naushad Ali and Pandit Shiv Kumar Sharma.

from start to finish. This is something unheard of and virtually impossible to achieve. Leave alone singing an entire verse, most songs today are recorded line by line. I feel blessed to have witnessed these miraculous recordings and I know her genius is no myth.

She has never taken her fame seriously. She often says public memory is short-lived and fame will fade someday. Her simplicity and humility will always set her apart from everyone.

A loosely translated verse by an anonymous Arabic poet beautifully summarises her life: 'Take from life all that is pure — and for living that is sufficient.' She is the only person I know who lives this verse. In her presence, I will always remain that beguiled child.

Radha Mangeshkar *niece*

Didi, to me, is not only the greatest artiste that history has ever seen, but also a grandmotherly figure to the entire family.

Musically, what can I or anyone say? She is the embodiment of 'swar' itself. In my little musical experience, never have I heard, whether live or in a recording, anyone as perfect as her. To me, she is the dictionary meaning of the word 'perfect.' She is an institution, a 'gharana.' I am proud to say she is the only artiste I listen to. And try in my own humble way to emulate. She is my guru.

She is the most generous person I have ever seen. She gladly gives away so many things to so many people. And she is equally generous when it comes to imparting the most precious of all riches: knowledge. She helps so many singers and composers better their work, without anyone having the slightest inkling that she is the silent contributor to so many wonderful creations.

She has brought me up like a princess, pampering me every moment of my life, yet she has also taught me the essence of life is simplicity in one's heart and behaviour.

I pray the hand that she has placed on my head to bless me — helps me to realise her dream of seeing a third generation of Mangeshkars sing well.

Radha (aged six) photographed by Lata Mangeshkar.

Awards

Government of India Awards

1969 Padma Bhushan

1989 Dada Saheb Phalke Award

1999 Padma Vibhushan

2001 Bharat Ratna, India's highest civilian award

2008 Lifetime Achievement Award on the occasion of the 60th anniversary of Independence

Maharashtra State Awards

1966 Best Playback Singer for *Sadhi Mansa*

Best Music Director for *Sadhi Mansa*

1967 Best Playback Singer for *Jait Re Jait*

2001 Maharashtra Ratna (First Recipient)

National Awards

1972 Best Female Playback Singer for *Parichay*

1975 Best Female Playback Singer for *Kora Kaagaz*

1990 Best Female Playback Singer for *Lekin*

Doctor of Letters

Shivaji University, India

Kolhapur University, India

Pune University, India

Khairagarh Music University, India

Hyderabad University, India

York University, Canada

Baroda University, India

Devi Ahilya University, India

Nagpur University, India

Goa University, India

Filmfare Awards

The *Filmfare* Awards for playback singing were initiated in 1958. In 1969, Lata Mangeshkar decided that in order to promote fresh talent she would no longer accept the *Filmfare* awards.

1958 'Aaja re pardesi' *(Madhumati)*

1962 'Kahin deep jale kahin dil *(Bees Saal Baad)*

1965 'Tumhin mere mandir tumhin meri pooja' *(Khandaan)*

1969 'Aap mujhe achhe lagne lage' *(Jeene ki Raah)*

1993 *Filmfare* Lifetime Achievement Award

1994 *Filmfare* Special Award for 'Didi tera dewar deewana' *(Hum Aapke Hai Koun…?)*

Other Awards and Honours

1974 Featured in the Guinness Book of World Records for having sung the maximum number of songs in the world

1980 Presented the key to the city of Georgetown, Guyana, South America

Honorary Citizenship of The Republic of Surinam, South America

1985 9th June, declared as Asia Day in honour of her arrival in Toronto, Canada

1987 Honorary Citizenship of USA in Houston, Texas

1990 Raja-Lakshmi Award by Sri Raja-Lakshmi Foundation, Chennai

1996 Videocon Screen Lifetime Achievement Award

1997 Rajiv Gandhi Award

1998 Lux Zee Cine Lifetime Achievement Award

1999 NTR National Award

2000 Lifetime Achievement Award by IIFA in London

Jeevan Gaurav Puraskar by the Chaturang Pratishthan

2001 Best Playback Singer of the Millennium (female) by Hero Honda and film magazine *Stardust*

Noorjehan Award (First Recipient)

2002 Felicitation By CII (For Contribution to Music & the Film Industry)

Hakim Khan Sur Award (For National Integration by Maharana Mewar Foundation)

Asha Bhosle Award (First Recipient)

2006 Knight of the Legion of Honour (France's highest civilian award)

Swar Bharati award given by Shankaracharya of Sankeshwar

The only Asian to have received the Platinum Disc by EMI London

Conferred the title of Asthaan Sangeet Vidwaan Sarloo (translation: Court Musician of the Shrine), Tirupathi.

Lata Mangeshkar was nominated Member of the Rajya Sabha in 1999. She has also received 250 trophies and 150 Gold Discs.

Bengal Film Journalist's Association Awards

Best Female Playback Singer for the following films:

1964 *Woh Kaun Thi*

1967 *Milan*

1968 *Raja Aur Rank*

Saraswatichandra

1970 *Do Raaste*

1971 *Tere Mere Sapne*

1973 *Marjina Abdulla* (Bengali)

Abhimaan

1975 *Kora Kagaaz*

1981 *Ek Dujje Ke Liye*

1983 *A Portrait of Lataji*

1985 *Ram Teri Ganga Maili*

The Lata Mangeshkar Award

The Lata Mangeshkar Award is a national-level award instituted by the State Government of Madhya Pradesh in 1984. The award consists of a certificate of merit and a cash award of 1 lakh rupees.

Award winners include:

Naushad Ali (1984)

Kishore Kumar (1985)

Jaidev (1986)

Manna Dey (1987)

Khayyam (1988)

Asha Bhosle (1989)

Bhupen Hazarika (2000)

Mahendra Kapoor (2002)

Sandhya Mukherjee (2003)

Snehal Bhatkar (2004)

Manna Dey (2005)

Jayamala Shiledar (2006)

A 'Lata Mangeshkar Award' was also initiated in 1992 by the Maharashtra Government. The award consists of a certificate of merit and a cash award of 1 lakh rupees. Lata Mangeshkar has sung in 36 languages. The majority of these songs were recorded, while others were performed live during stage shows.

She has sung the greatest number of songs in:

Marathi *(mother tongue)*

Hindi

Urdu

Sanskrit

The others (in alphabetical order) are:

Assamese
Awadhi
Bengali
Bhojpuri
Brij Bhasa
Chhattisgarhi
Dogri
English
Fijian
Gujarati
Gurmukhi
Kannada
Kashmiri
Konkani
Latin
Magadhi
Maithili
Malayalam
Manipuri
Marwari
Nepali
Oriya
Prakrit (Jain *shlok*)
Punjabi
Rajasthani
Russian
Sindhi
Sinhali
Surinami
Swahili
Tamil
Telugu

In 1969, she received the Padma Bhushan from the President of India, Dr. Zakir Husain.

In 1999, she received the Padma Vibhushan from the President of India, K.R. Narayanan.

Atal Bihari Vajpayee at the release of the album Antar Naad *[Inner Voice], featuring the former Prime Minister's poems set to music and sung by Lata Mangeshkar. She regards Atalji as a father figure. At this occasion, she wittily said that if we read the name 'Atal' backwards, it is in fact 'Lata.'*

Lata Mangeshkar was conferred the Bharat Ratna, the nation's highest civilian honour, by President K.R. Narayanan. 2001.

HMV Studios, Bombay. Photo credit: Gautam Rajadhyaksha.

(top) Sachin Tendulkar, Lata Mangeshkar, Amitabh Bachchan and Balasaheb Thackeray at a fundraising event held on March, 2001, for the victims of the Gujarat earthquake. Now rarely performing in public, she sang at the fundraiser. Bottom left: With Richard Gere. Middle: With Sachin Tendulkar and Shah Rukh Khan. Bottom right: Aamir Khan receiving the Deenanath Mangeshkar Award. April, 2008.

A rare family portrait taken at niece Rachana's marriage to Dr. Nishit Shah in Bombay, on 2nd February, 1990. First row (kneeling, left to right): nephew Yogesh, niece Radha, Dr. Nishit Shah, Rachana, and nephews Adinath and Baijnath. Second row (left to right): Hridaynath, his wife, Bharati, Lataji, her mother, sisters Asha, Usha and Meena, Anuja Bhosle, wife of nephew Anand (and standing next to him) is niece Varsha. Back row (left to right): guest, Avinash Mohite (Deenanath Mangeshkar's disciple) Mr. Khadikar, nephew Hemant Bhosle and his daughter Anika and wife Sajida.

The Mangeshkar family at Adinath's marriage to Krishna in 2005.

Photograph by Lata Mangeshkar.

Facing page *Lyrics: Majrooh Sultanpuri*
Music: Madan Mohan
Film: Baaghi *(1953)*

हमारे बाद अब महफ़िल में अफ़साने बयाँ होंगे
बहारें हम को ढूंढेंगी न जाने हम कहाँ होंगे...

Hamaare baad ab mehfil mein afsaane bayaan honge
Bahaaren hum ko dhoondengi na jaane hum kahaan honge...

When I am gone, the world may speak of me
The spring will seek me out, but who knows where I will be...

Glossary

alaap	*literally a dialogue or conversation; in music it denotes a conversation between the musician and the* raag*. It starts with the key note* 'Sa,' *is slow in tempo, has no lyrics and is not accompanied by any drum*
amrut sparsh	*touch that renders a person immortal*
antara	*second part of a composition, showing the upper register*
ashram	*retreat, hermitage or monastery; the place where a guru resides with his disciples*
asthayi	*also known as* sthayi*; the first part of a composition, which is often repeated and rarely consists of notes of the upper register*
bandish	*melodic composition set to a particular* raag*, usually consisting of two parts: the* asthayi *and* antara
bhajan	*type of Hindu devotional song expressing love for the Divine. The lyrics are simple and the music is sometimes based on classical* raags*. Bhajans of Kabir, Meerabai, Surdas and Tulsidas are classic examples*
bhavgeet	*form of music in which poems, mostly romantic in nature, are set to melodious tunes. The base of the tunes may be classical, but the tone is never heavy and is either light or semi-classical*
bhel	*snack consisting of puffed rice served in a spicy sauce with onion, coriander and other condiments, often sold on Mumbai's beaches and at roadside food stalls*
chhatai	*a rug usually made of grass or coir, traditionally spread on the floor for sitting*
dilruba	*popular bowed instrument of Northern India having 18 or 19 elliptical frets, 4 main strings and around 22 sympathetic strings running under the frets tied to pegs on the sides. While playing, the instrument is held vertically on one's lap with the upper body resting against one's shoulder; the bow is held in the right hand and the strings are pressed with the fingers of the left hand.*
dholak	*traditionally played at marriages, it is a classical North Indian hand drum with a cylindrical shell made of* shisham *wood. Its right-hand side has a simple membrane and a handle while its left-hand membrane is covered with a coating of clay, tar and sand, modifying pitch and tone*
dhoop	*incense*
doha	*two-line love song or mystical song often associated with the Bhakti saint-poet Kabir (1290-1410?)*
filmi	*style related to commercial Indian films, sometimes denoting melodramatic or flashy*
gandha	*thread tied by the guru/teacher on the wrist of his/her disciple signifying acceptance to teach the disciple*
gandhar	*denotes* 'Ga,' *the third of the seven notes that make up Indian classical music*
ghagra-choli	*Rajasthani costume consisting of a long skirt, blouse and a cloth (scarf/veil) to cover the head*
ghamak taan	*type of* taan *where a single note is reverberated for emphasis*

gharana	*stylistic tradition or school of thought by which a particular musical style is preserved by its members and passed down from one generation to the next*
ghazal	*conversing with the beloved; Urdu poem consisting of 5 to 25 couplets in which the last verse often features the pen name of the poet*
gilli-danda	*amateur sport popular in North India played with two wooden sticks, the shorter stick is called* gilli *and the longer,* danda, *resembling a cricket bat and ball*
gote	*traditional Maharashtrian bracelet*
harkat	*stylistic variation of a* taan *rendering a composition more appealing, demonstrating the performer's expertise and control of the characteristic features of the* raag *and its* swaras
kathak	*classical dance form of North India; its name is derived from the term* 'katha' *meaning story. Hence it is a narrative dance form and is characterised by the* tatkar *(fast footwork),* chakkar *(spins) and a unique combination of* bhav *(feelings, mood) and* abhinaya *(expression)*
khayal	*'thought'; form of Indian classical vocal music, in which the Urdu lyrics have great emotional significance and are performed in a particular* raag *by the singer*
khola	*kettle drum*
kirtan	*devotional songs that originally emerged from the Bhakti movement of 15th-century India. These simple melodies are most often sung as a chorus, accompanied by handclaps, finger cymbals and drums*
kurta-pyjama	*loose-fitting collarless shirt and draw-stringed trousers*
laddoo	*round shaped Indian sweet made of lentils*
mandir	*altar; temple*
maulana	*Arabic word, literally meaning 'Lord'; an address to one's master (or teacher) used as a title in Central Asia and the Indian subcontinent*
mehfil	*soiree or informal gathering. In Muslim literary 'culture,' it often refers to a gathering of poets*
mujra	*form of dance, usually performed by courtesans*
murki	*quivering of several notes around a central note*
naat	*song in praise of the Prophet Mohammed*
namaskar	*greeting or salutation; literally, 'I bow to you'*
paan	*betel leaf wrapped around areca nuts. It is offered as a mark of hospitality and often eaten after a meal as a digestive*
paatli	*traditional Maharashtrian bracelet*
pasanda	*lamb Mughlai delicacy, which can be served both as a meat dish or kebab*
payal	*anklet*
praman	*true to life*
pulao	*rice dish cooked in clarified butter with whole spices and dry fruits*
qawali	*form of Sufi devotional song, usually sung in Urdu or Punjabi*
raag	*combination of several notes denoting a particular mood in Indian classical music and pertaining to a specific time of the day/season*

rakhi	*thread tied by a sister on the wrist of her brother or any male who then becomes an 'adopted' brother, denoting a bond of brotherly protection*
roti	*type of Indian unleavened bread*
sangeet natak	*musical play*
sarangi	*short-necked bowed instrument carved out of a single wood piece. It consists of 3 main strings and a diatonic row of 9* tarabs *(resonance strings) and a chromatic one of 15 tarabs. Of all instruments, the sound of the sarangi is said to have the greatest resemblance to the human voice*
sargam	*collection of notes or* swaras, *namely* Sa, Ri *(Carnatic) or* Re *(Hindustani),* Ga, Ma, Pa, Da *(Carnatic) or* Dha *(Hindustani), and* Ni. *The word* 'sargam' *is formed by the consonants of the first four notes*
sarod	*stringed lute-like instrument which has 4 to 6 main melodic strings, and 2 to 4 additional strings. The player holds the instrument across his lap, plays with a plectrum held in the right hand, while pressing the strings with the fingernails of his left hand*
shagird	*Urdu for 'disciple'*
shehnai	*wind instrument like the flute, considered auspicious, hence played at marriages and on religious occasions. It has become a popular instrument of classical music in the recent past*
shlok	*Sanskrit term denoting a metered, often rhymed poetic verse or phrase; it is the chief metre used in the epics Mahabharat and Ramayan, and has come to mean a proverb or hymn of praise to be sung or chanted in liturgy*
sureelapan	*melodiousness*
swar	*pitch; note; melody*
taal	*beat which determines the rhythmic structure of a composition*
taan	*metered run of musical notes following a particular tempo and specific to a* raag
taanga	*horse-drawn carriage*
tandoori	*food cooked or baked over charcoal or wood in a* tandoor, *a cylindrical clay-oven heated to a high temperature*
tanpura	*long-necked stringed instrument of North India resembling a sitar and played as accompaniment. It has no frets, only 4 or 5 wire strings which are plucked one after another to provide a harmonic resonance to the basic note*
thumri	*form of Indian semi-classical music denoting a song having an attractive, rather sensuous, melody and rhythm. It often projects the various romantic moods of union and separation*

Compiled by Madhuparna Banerjee

Index

Page numbers followed by "f" indicate figures/photographs.

C

H

I

J

L

M

N

O

T